D0849562

FROM THE EDITORS OF ESQUIRE MAGAZINE

The Handbook of Style

A MAN'S GUIDE TO LOOKING GOOD

Esquire

HEARST BOOKS

A Division of Sterling Publishing Co., Inc.

New York / London

www.sterlingpublishing.com

The Contents

FOREWORD

WE HATE TO BE TOLD WHAT TO DO. It's part of being a man. We bridle at authority. We resent rules. Or we don't believe they apply to us. A cop pulls us over; a television doctor tells us how to better take care of ourselves; the pinhead from the TSA tells us to take our belt off. Our kneejerk is to give *him* a little advice.

SO, IN THIS BOOK, we're not telling you what to do. I promise. We have opinions, yes. Some of us have experience. All of us care about how a man presents himself to the world. We share a belief that even a modicum of effort—in dressing, in interpersonal interaction, in being a good friend or colleague or lover—pays huge dividends.

AND THAT IS what this book is about. Yes, it's a guide to how to get dressed and it is a primer on the elements of style, but by no means is it a set of unbending rules. There are people who, through the many centuries during which men have chosen to put on clothes, have offered specific dictates that they expected to be followed specifically.

BUT THAT IS NOT US. Consider what we offer here recommendations. Even when we speak with certainty, understand that nothing is intended as absolute. We don't truck in rules. We make suggestions based on our experiences, our understanding of the history of how men get dressed and our keen observation of our fellow men. Nothing is immutable. One of the disappointments of our age is that men have no mentors in the arts of style. Our fathers, raised too late in the twentieth century to have been allowed to prize style, had nothing to pass on to us. Or they were turned away by the impatience of our younger selves. We, for the most part, were on our own, made the mistakes of youth, and muddled through.

THE INTENTION of this book is to give you a sense of not only the how but the why. To explain to you not just that certain types of shoes work best for certain social events but what the history of that shoe is and a strategy for negotiating the intricacies of the social event to which you will be wearing it.

FOR SEVENTY-FIVE YEARS, *Esquire* has offered men advice on how to make their ways through the world as easily and successfully as possible. Some of what we know we learned from our editorial forebears and from the archetypes of men's style they learned from. But some of it has been learned in our journeys through the streets of Naples, where men dress with imagination, and into the basements of Savile Row, where tailors work, and while we are out late in Manhattan, marveling at the lightness with which the American version of style rests on our shoulders.

THIS IS A BOOK of suggestions. We mean them and expect you to learn from them things that work for you. But you will transgress them, and in that transgression you will make choices that will make us proud to know you.

David Granger
Editor-in-Chief, Esquire

Introduction

THIS BOOK IS A ROAD MAP FOR A TERRITORY
that's familiar and strange at the same time. The landscape
of style is forever shifting, but its permanent features
encompass both classic clothing and the finer points of living
well. We'll show you the lay of the land, point out acceptable
detours from the straight-and-narrow, warn against the
proverbial tourist traps, and hope to send you on your way
with a good sense of direction and a can-do attitude.

LIKE ANY MAPPING project, this book builds on an earlier survey, *The Big
Black Book*, published annually to great success by Esquire beginning in 2006.
We're told by reputable sources that men are regularly observed perusing
its pages and comparing notes in business-class. Maybe you are one of them.
Clearly, we figured, there is a yearning for instruction, particularly in the
value of choosing well. We decided that a more compact book—like-minded
in approach, with no-nonsense illustrations, comprehensive and focusing
on pragmatics—was in order. Taking the *Big Black Book*'s information pages
as its cue, this *Handbook of Style* breaks down the male wardrobe into
its constituent parts and dedicates one chapter to each: suits, shirts and
sweaters, trousers, shoes and boots, coats and outerwear, and accessories—
with an additional chapter on personal care.

OUR MANTRA IS that you don't need more clothes, you need better clothes, and these chapters offer advice on how to acquire the finest quality gear you can afford. They also explain why these pieces work well together and suggest when it's appropriate to wear them. Each chapter is organized roughly from the general to the specific, beginning with a short introduction. From there we proceed to the best basics for your wardrobe and build; and from there to short how-to's on specific styles, fabrics, and materials. Each chapter concludes with pointers about storing and caring for your clothes once you have them, because although the idea of a personal valet at the ready with pressed trousers and a hangover cure at 8:00 a.m. seems irreproachable, we're betting that few of you have your own Jeeves at home. (Grandmothers who darn socks, and wives—or husbands, for that matter—willing to hand wash sweaters are also in short supply these days.)

FINALLY, WE'VE INCLUDED a page at the end of each chapter called "The Sartorial Canon," which presents an entirely selective list of some of our favorite haberdashers—those who have persisted in offering consummate quality and taste, often through several centuries and the turbulence of fashion. You won't be excommunicated from the style council if your closet doesn't include a piece from one of these venerable manufacturers, but if you're stuck at a fashion crossroads, you'll generally never go wrong by choosing one, either.

OF COURSE, IT doesn't matter how polished the individual items in your wardrobe are if you can't pull them into a coherent, signature look. One way to develop sartorial aplomb is by looking at how style icons, past and present, did it. You'll see a lot of them in these pages; we're calling them "The Originals." Fred Astaire, Cary Grant, Marlon Brando, Frank Sinatra, George Clooney, André 3000: these are men who turn almost any combination of clothes, from the simplest white T-shirt and five-pocket jeans to the most sophisticated Savile Row suit, into a striking, but hardly ever ostentatious, personal statement.

WHAT ALL THESE illustrious guys have in common is taste. Not boring, I-followed-the-rules "good" taste, but risky, I-tossed-the-rules-I-didn't-like taste. Which, in the end, is the only sort of taste that counts: informed, fearless, unapologetic, personal. Don't think it was always an easy matter for the sharp dressers we've chosen; often, they only got to look so cool by giving their attire a lot of careful thought.

CASE IN POINT: Sinatra, the scrawny kid from Hoboken turned Palm Springs dandy, took as much professional pride in his appearance as he did in his recordings, continually refining both until his look and his sound seemed effortless. Sinatra gave instructions to the centimeter on the length of his collar points and the break in his trousers. He made stylishness appear both manly and easy. Even Brando, the poster boy for couldn't-give-a-damn insouciance, developed enough cocky sartorial smarts to know that his T-shirts and black-leather motorcycle jackets were more flattering on him than expensive tailoring would be. (The famous torn T-shirt that Stanley wears in *A Streetcar Named Desire* was simply Brando's rehearsal garb.)

THE GREAT STYLE icons are inspirational in two senses: They show us how to pull off a truly personal look and why it's a worthwhile goal in the first place. Dressing well is a way of integrating and expressing your personality; it's a way of finding out about yourself and expressing that knowledge to the world at large. It may not be as complex or revelatory as making a painting or writing a book, but it's an honest, meaningful method of distinguishing yourself from the pack. And when you're heading out on your own, it's always best to carry a map.

CHAPTER ONE

The Suit

SINCE THE TIME IT WAS INTRODUCED
in the seventeenth century, the modern suit has been about two things: power and sex. If you doubt us, try this simple experiment. Some evening, go to a nice hotel bar where you don't know anyone, wearing jeans and a T-shirt. ➤

THE JEANS DON'T EVEN have to have holes in them, and the T-shirt can be clean. Now, return to the same bar the next evening wearing a nice suit. Take note of the difference in the reactions of the bartender and of the other patrons in the bar. Remember them. Write them down if you must.

THUS YOU SEE how a sleek, well-cut suit can turn everyman into the ideal man: serious, powerful, physically charismatic. For this we thank Beau Brummel, the legendary Regency-era dandy who turned his back on the flamboyantly beribboned men's fashion of the previous centuries and instead embraced perfectly tailored, neutrally colored pieces in luxury fabrics like linen and chamois leather. Brummel became the talk of the town for his sartorial derring-do (and for the unheard-of habit of bathing daily), but his m.o. works as well today as it did two hundred years ago: good taste and style are best expressed by an impeccably tailored, elegant suit on a fit, clean body.

BRUMMEL'S RENEGADE APPROACH was bolstered by the neoclassical revival, which introduced a new masculine physical ideal: the Greek athlete, with a torso in the shape of an inverted triangle. Deft English tailors transformed the plain wool coat, waistcoat, and breeches of the country gentleman into an elegantly molded, comfortable urban garment that gave its wearer what appeared to be the physique of a classical sculpture. It didn't take long for the middle class to figure out that what the suit did for the landed gentry it could do for them, and once democratizing ready-to-wear garments were introduced in the mid-nineteenth century, would-be fine gentlemen emerged everywhere.

AT THE BEGINNING of the twentieth century, Neapolitan tailors, impressed by the high-style Edwardian clothing of vacationing British nobs, mastered the tricks of the London suit-making trade. But they modified the construction techniques to produce a supple, weightless, unlined *giacca* that is relaxed and comfortable in Naples's hot climate. Giorgio Armani successfully adapted the loose-jointed Neapolitan suit in the 1970s. He gave it a fuller cut and a distinctive Milanese slouch that dominated the stylish man's wardrobe for the next decade, famously appearing on Richard Gere in *American Gigolo* in 1980.

THE ARMANI LOOK was a more sophisticated version of the American "sack" suit. Introduced around the turn of the twentieth century, the shapeless suit soon became the universal business uniform and, mass-produced in gray flannel, the very symbol of white-collar conformity. A favorite of Ivy Leaguers and mid-level corporate strivers during the Eisenhower era, its hegemony was challenged by the relatively snappy navy blue two-button suits of President John F. Kennedy, and by the slim-blade, dark-and-narrow ensembles worn by the cast of the original 1960 film *Ocean's Eleven*. The Rat Pack suit was called the Continental look, and it originated in Rome; it's what the disaffected charmers wear in the movies of Fellini and Antonioni.

WHILE IMAGES OF the Rat Pack are fresh in your mind, let's consider another staple of their wardrobe: the tuxedo. In all likelihood, this is not a garment that you will be called upon to wear often, unless you are a classical musician or a professional partygoer. But there is no substitute for possessing your own if you can afford it. Find your style and wear it, and you're instantly part of a rarefied and elegant tradition. And what tradition involving Champagne, caviar, and women in backless gowns could be all bad?

SINCE NO ONE has yet devised a plausible replacement for formal male dress, the only way to fight the suit's lingering aura of conventionality has been to play obsessively with its fabric, details, and silhouette. Given the body consciousness that has pervaded popular culture since the 1980s, it's not surprising that a slimmed-down cut is enjoying a moment in the fashion spotlight. (Of course, there's only so much paunch that a pared-down jacket can disguise). But a recent trend—the shrunken suit, featuring a short, tight jacket and ankle-baring pants—removes all business-world connotations from the tailored garment, making it appealing to hipsters who never set foot in an office. It, too, derives from the Continental look, but by way of the Mods— 1960s British scenesters who rode Vespas and wore the pants of their snug Italian mohair suits too short. No one ever mistook them for bankers, either.

DAVID GRANGER on
HOW TO DRESS WELL

FIRST, YOU HAVE TO WANT TO. At some point in my tenure as a sportswriter, I figured out why big-time athletes disdain the vast majority of reporters. It wasn't because we were small and weak. It wasn't because we asked impolite questions and wrote articles they didn't like. No. It was because we dressed like hell. I came to this conclusion after seeing a photo of myself sitting in the Cincinnati Reds' dugout interviewing their star slugger. I can still see the blue short-sleeved checked shirt I was wearing in that photo. I can still feel the rush of humiliation I felt when I realized that the superstar must have looked at me for the first time and immediately thought to himself: *writer*. He lumped me in. And he wasn't wrong to do so.

It's hard to be successful if you're lumped in, if you're one of the many. You can get along, for sure. Bureaucrats get along. But dressing—style—is about standing out; it's about making a subtle statement, and that statement is simply: "I'm different." You can't be so outlandish that the statement is read as either "I'm better" or "I'm an asshole." There's a fine line. Nick Sullivan, *Esquire*'s fashion director, has a phrase he uses to describe what it is we're talking about: the Extra 10 Percent.

There's some guidance on these pages, but the secret to dressing a little better is simply this: You have to want to. If you don't, it's just not going to be part of your life. And that's not a terrible thing. Style is a gentle act of will. I remember when

I started to care. I bought a few things—things I could afford. A couple of dark suits, some nice shirts—mostly white at first, then some stripes. Some basic ties—a black knit, a gray-and-dark-gray repp. But nothing mattered until the morning I stood in front of my closet and *thought* about what I was going to wear.

On that morning, or one soon after, I remember looking at my humble wardrobe and wanting to try something I had never tried before. I don't remember what the combination was, but it was an important moment. It opened up possibilities. I no longer had *outfits*. I had *options*. For a while I tried dressing in threes: two patterns and a texture. I discovered that the simplest way to make people think you look sharp is to dress in black and white, especially a black suit, white-white shirt with French cuffs, and white-white pocket square. For various six-month periods, I've entirely eschewed the tie, only to adopt it anew when the season changes. There are millions of rules. (Always wear white to the face. The turtleneck is the most flattering thing a man can wear.) And those rules need to be accepted and then, on a case-by-case basis, modified or rejected.

I failed a lot and I still fail. Sometimes I get to the office, after dressing in the near dark of early morning, and I think, *This* is what I'm wearing? But what the stink? It's a day in the life. Tomorrow, I'll spend my ninety seconds in contemplation and move on.

HUMPHREY BOGART AND THE TWEED SUIT

➤ *While Humphrey Bogart came to epitomize 1940s Hollywood and the romantic tough-guy, in his personal life he preferred to play, and dress, the part of Continental country gentleman. In a brilliantly tailored tweed suit with notched lapels and patch pockets, Bogie here looks more Duke of Windsor than African Queen. Perfect for a life of patrician leisure on his European-style estate in L.A. with his wife, actress Lauren Bacall.*

The **PERFECT SUIT**

The only one you need for work, weddings, funerals, parties, and everything in between

➤ NATURAL SHOULDER

Keep it fairly natural—too much padding makes the suit look like it's wearing you.

➤ NOTCHED LAPEL

Your lapel speaks volumes. A small, high notch right on the collarbone is the mark of a killer suit, a minor detail that makes your off-the-peg suit look closer to classic bespoke.

➤ DEEP NAVY, WOOL CLOTH

It's dark enough to appear professional, but also lighter and classier than rather dour black. Lightweight wool stands up best to repeated wearing and can be worn year-round. An interesting texture like hopsack, or even a small-scale herringbone weave, lends some subtle depth to an otherwise simple suit.

➤ FITTED WAIST

The jacket should have some fit to it in the waist area to give your body a more dynamic shape.

➤ SIMPLICITY

The more streamlined the details, the more widely you will be able to wear it. Avoid extra pockets and flamboyant stitch detailing.

➤ TROUSERS

Flat-front trousers are considered more modern, but pleats will be a touch more forgiving should your waistline expand over time. A cuff's added weight keeps your pant creases sharper. A cuff should be between one and a half and one and three-quarters inches in height.

THE TERMS: JACKETOLOGY

•

Six obscure bits of suit jargon you may never need to use but might be glad to know all the same.

THE DROP: The term used to denote a suit's shape, e.g., a "drop six" means a trouser waist six inches smaller than the chest.

THE JIGGER: The single button in a double-breasted jacket that is always kept fastened.

BOSOM POCKET: Pockets cut into the suit's fabric, usually covered with a flap.

TICKET POCKET: The third pocket above the side pocket of a jacket (normally the right one), usually with a flap.

KISSING BUTTONS: How cuff buttons on expensive suits are sewn so they almost overlap up the sleeve.

THE SCYE: The term for the armhole, the size and shape of which often determine the jacket's fit.

THE DEFINITIVE STYLE RULES

NAVY SUITS

1. A navy suit can be worn with both black and brown belts and shoes. A black suit cannot.

2. The best shoe color for a navy suit: chocolate brown. It's dark enough to wear at night and colorful enough to shine during the day.

3. Tuck in your shirt.

4. Three things you need in that party shirt underneath your navy suit: big cuffs, a high collar, and quality pearl buttons. One thing you don't: bling.

5. Navy doesn't have to mean plain. Instead of toying with loud stripes, try a textured fabric to give your navy suit added character.

6. Two expensive suits are better than five cheap ones. One of them should be navy.

7. The John Kruk rule: Know your neck size. (He obviously doesn't.) You should be able to fit one finger between your collar and your neck when your shirt is fully buttoned.

8. Neurotic comedians like Richard Lewis wear only black. Do not follow suit.

THE NAVY SUIT

Four Different Ways

You won't find any-
thing more versatile,
more worth the
investment, than a
great navy suit. It's
the utility infielder
of a man's closet,
keeping you sharp
whether you're
eyeing a spot at the
bar or a seat on the
board. Think classic
two-button, with
a subtle texture
and a tailored fit.
The jacket can also
work as a free agent
paired with other
pants in your closet,
because the secret to
a flexible wardrobe
is wearing clothes
of such undeniable
quality that they'll
work in any scenario.
And a good navy suit
will do just that.

For Sunday afternoon
*A lightweight sweater
underneath the jacket,
matched with a pair of
corduroy pants, keeps
things casual but still sharp.*

For Monday morning
*Sure, you've got to button
up for the boss and a client
meeting, but bold stripes
and French cuffs preserve
your individuality.*

For Thursday night
*The shirt's subtle yet
colorful stripes, French
cuffs, and high, thick collar
make it the perfect party
shirt to complement the
suit's fitted silhouette.*

For Fridays
*A classic three-button,
with a subtle texture and a
tailored fit. Ditch the pants
and pair the jacket with
khakis, corduroys, or a pair
of dark jeans.*

THE FOUR ESSENTIAL SUITS

What every man needs, in the order he needs it

THE STAPLE	THE SPARE

Start with navy blue (see pp. 19–21). It's formal enough for all manner of buttoned-up business, and it's much classier than black.	Add some variety with a light gray suit, and opt for a lightweight worsted rather than wintry flannel.
THE PINSTRIPE	*THE BOLDER CHECK*

Ease your way into patterns with a fine pinstripe. It's always in style, and as a bonus for the short of height (if not stature), the vertical lines make you look taller.	Now for some fun. Get creative with patterns like this classic glen plaid; it adds texture and depth to your closet.

PEE-WEE HERMAN AND THE SHRUNKEN SUIT

➡ *Seems it's always the weirdos who push the boundaries of style. Shrink-wrapped in his gray polyester suit, Pee-wee Herman was a beguiling blend of the nerdish and the knowing, a spiffily dressed man-child who refused to grow up. Who knew that the trim-fitting, ankle-bearing style of the guy who spoke to armchairs would be strutting down New York runways twenty years later? Goes to show you: sometimes it's hip to be square.*

THE SECRET CODE
• OF BUTTONS •

BUTTON
UNBUTTON

ONE-
BUTTON

TWO-
BUTTON

THREE-
BUTTON

DOUBLE-
BREASTED

VEST

{ *The RULES* }

•

*THE INJUSTICE IN
THE 2005 NBA DRESS*
code is that it did not
ban five-button suits.

•

*UNBUTTONING THE
BUTTONS ON YOUR
JACKET SLEEVE*
only proves you're a
show-off.

Buttons and You
A Handy Guide

THE SHORT GUY
Lengthen your
silhouette by choosing a
one-button jacket with
natural shoulders. The
deep V will give length
to your torso.

THE SKINNY GUY
A double-breasted jacket
gives more width to a
slim torso. The button
stance and the extra
cloth add bulk.

THE BROAD GUY
A two-button jacket
gives a slimming effect
similar to a one-button
jacket, with a deep V
between the lapels to
lengthen the torso.

THE BIG AND TALL GUY
A three-button suit has
the shortest V of all.
Its fit should be close
and comfortable.

THE MATH ON

The Double-Breasted Suit

The three types of classic double-breasted jackets are determined by the number of buttons. For all styles, the lapels are always peaked and the jacket always buttoned, never left open to flap in the breeze à la *David Letterman.*

"THE SIX-ON-ONE"
Six buttons, of which only the bottom right-hand side button is functional. This style, popularized by the Duke of Kent in the 1930s, has a long, rolled lapel and a wider, lower gorge that exposes more of the shirt and tie. Some people think this creates a longer line that's flattering on shorter men.

"THE SIX-ON-TWO"
Six buttons, of which only the center and bottom right-hand side buttons are functional. Only the center button is used; the lowest button is always left undone. Although this is the most traditional of double-breasted styles, its high, tight gorge looks crisp and modern.

"THE SIX-ON-SIX"
Six buttons, of which all three left-hand side buttons are functional. All buttons are usually done up, creating a very high, tight gorge. A rather military or naval style, it's most often found in traditional blazers with metal buttons; in suits, it floats in and out with the fashion tide.

"THE FOUR-ON-ONE"
Four buttons, of which only the bottom right-hand side button is functional. Because the button stance is higher on the jacket than a six-button configuration, the gorge normally lies somewhere between the lower six-on-one and the higher six-on-two.

AL CAPONE AND THE PINSTRIPE SUIT
➥ *When Prohibition turned gangsters into businessmen and Al Capone adopted the suit traditionally worn by bankers (then examples of upstanding citizenry), little did he know that one day he'd be trading pinstripes for jail stripes. The exaggerated stripes, shoulders, and lapels that Capone favored gave the suit a wise-guy aura it's never totally shaken. Still, in restrained form, the pinstripe is fit for a president. On a savvy mogul like Sean Combs, its banker-bandit ambiguity lends valuable street cred.*

THE NINE PATTERNS YOU SHOULD KNOW

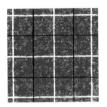

1. WINDOWPANE
Good for: Business suits that moonlight as party wear.

2. HOUNDSTOOTH
Good for:
Bold jackets and suits for special occasions.

3. CHALK-STRIPE FLANNEL
Good for: Hearty cold-weather suits that mean business.

4. PINSTRIPE WORSTED
Good for: Business of any kind.

5. BIRD'S EYE
Good for: Cocktail suits that women always seem to notice.

6. HERRINGBONE
Good for: Casual blazers and cold-weather trousers.

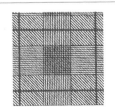

7. GLEN PLAID
Good for:
Classic suits for the office.

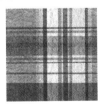

8. MADRAS
Good for: Warm-weather blazers paired with jeans.

9. SEERSUCKER
Good for: Suits and pants that look sharp in torrid heat.

Jackets and Patterns: A Field Guide

Because man cannot survive on solid colors alone

Patterned tie, striped shirt: This pairing looks best with plain jackets or mélange flannels.

Striped tie, striped shirt: The tie's stripes should always be bolder than the shirt's.

Checked shirt, striped jacket: The shirt's checks should be as big in scale as the jacket's stripes.

Checked jacket, knit tie: Match a visual texture (a check) with a tactile texture (knitted silk).

Striped jacket, striped shirt: The shirt's stripes should always appear bolder than the suit's.

Bold-check jacket, plain shirt: The bolder the check, the plainer the shirt.

Patterned jacket, striped shirt: Contrast the shirt's stripes with a fine-patterned suit.

Flannel jacket, checked shirt: The bolder the shirt check, the plainer the suit cloth.

> I KEPT THE SAME SUIT FOR SIX YEARS AND THE SAME DIALOGUE. THEY JUST CHANGED THE TITLE OF THE PICTURE AND THE LEADING LADY.
>
> *—Robert Mitchum*

{ *The* CLASSICS }
The Tweed Sport Coat

BEFORE GORE-TEX, before Polartec and micro-fleece, there was . . . the tweed sport coat? Robust and hard wearing, tweed's popularity grew out of the English obsession with Scotland that reached a mania with Queen Victoria and her husband, Prince Albert, in the mid-1800s. Wealthy new industrialists from the south began buying up castles and land from impoverished Scottish owners for the newly popular sports of grouse shooting and deerstalking, for which tweed was the requisite uniform. Tweed was also the fabric of choice for the upper-echelon Englishmen who founded the Alpine Club in 1857. They wore tweed sport coats—most notably Norfolk jackets, with numerous pockets to hold all of their climbing gadgets—and tweed breeches. In America the tweed sport coat came to symbolize the WASP in all his Ivy League splendor, and then became a semaphore for all-purpose bookishness (think Woody Allen). But the professorial uniform need not look fusty: worn with stylish twill jeans or a bold striped shirt, it's a solid anchor of good taste.

THE THREE
JACKET SHOULDERS

NATURAL
It looks like:
The Roman Empire – a gradual, stately decline. **Why you should wear it:** *Shows off, rather than hides, your body shape. Tailors prefer it.*

ROPED
It looks like: *The top of the sleeve is laid over a piece of rope. (It isn't.)* **Why you should wear it:** *Conveys a rigorous formality and a little old-school glamour.*

PADDED
It looks like: *You're a comedian from the 1980s.* **Why you should wear it:** *You're slight and could use more implied lateral bulk.*

{ *The* RULES }
•
A WARDROBE REQUIRES ONLY TWO BLAZERS.
The navy two-button blazer is the most functional—it can be dressed up with a tie or down with jeans. The lightweight tweed works for the weekend or any event at which there's a chance of having a conversation about the films of Wim Wenders.

TOM WOLFE AND THE WHITE SUIT

➤ *Like fellow southern clotheshorse Mark Twain, dandy author Tom Wolfe plucked the white suit off the plantation porch and made it the signature look in a dramatic urban wardrobe. His first white suit, purchased one summer in the early 1960s upon his arrival in New York, conferred instant personality on the relatively unknown Wolfe. No one since has pulled off the white suit so successfully, though Don Johnson gave it a shot in the 1980s, preening his way around the pastel world of* Miami Vice.

THE FORGOTTEN SEASON

THE SUMMER SUIT MANUAL

Maybe it's because we're used to stretching that wool suit we spent so much money on last fall as far as it can possibly go that summer somehow falls by the sartorial wayside. It's doomed to be the forgotten season. But it shouldn't be, because there are options. Cases in point: lightweight combinations like these. The light colors and breathable fabrics are made especially for hot July afternoons. They are also proof that even though some of us have forgotten how to dress between May and September, there are still clothes suited to the season. And we should take advantage of them.

WHITE

You don't have to be Tom Wolfe to pull off a white suit, especially if you match it with a patterned shirt and modern tie.

SEERSUCKER

To avoid looking like a dandy, you can dress a seersucker suit down and make it more modern by wearing a light-colored linen sweater underneath.

KHAKI

Khaki begs to be dressed up. Try layering it with a light sweater over a smart shirt and tie, finishing with, of course, a pocket square.

ALL IT TAKES ARE A FEW SIMPLE OUTFITS.
AND THERE'S ONE SECRET—THE SIMPLER THE BETTER.

—Cary Grant

THE MYSTERIES OF
SUMMER DRESSING—SOLVED

Frequently Asked Questions

Q Which color is least suited to summer?
We know black is cool, but sweating bullets isn't. Try light gray, khaki, or stone as alternatives.

Q Why should I wear wool in the summer?
Ask any desert dweller: The most comfortable fabric in extreme hot or cold is wool, which regulates body temperature. In its thinnest form (called Super 100's), wool drapes beautifully, breathes easily, and stretches, thanks to the natural elasticity of the fibers. Any creases from normal wear will fall out after the suit is removed and hung up; you can't say that for cotton or linen.

Q What's the deal with the seersucker suit, and what do I wear with it?

The cloth derives its name from the eighteenth-century term *sea sucker*. The suit should be matched with a light-colored shirt or sweater (when worn improperly, it evokes images of sweaty, overweight criminal-defense lawyers from Mississippi). Be sure that the rest of your accessories (belt, watchband, tie) play along—leave the pinkie ring, the .357, and the bankroll of hundreds at home. Finally, the seersucker suit is not an excuse to wear shoes without socks—match them to either stripe.

Q But is it okay to not wear socks in the summer?
Maybe. Just remember to give your poor sweaty shoes a break every other day.

Q Speaking of shoes, what sort might I wear with a cream or ivory suit, assuming

I don't want to look like Guido the Killer Pimp?
Pimps don't wear cotton, so we assume that you mean a cream-colored linen or silk-and-linen suit and that you're looking to tone down its dandyism. A pair of natural-leather wing tips will lessen the heady snazz of the suit and draw on its classic southern-gentleman style.

Q How did the summer suit get its start?
With the New Deal, which gave men more cash to spend on the forgotten season.

Q Any dressing don'ts I need to know?
Absolutely. Summer is *not* the perfect time to break out the Hawaiian prints from your honeymoon. Nor are jean shorts acceptable. And those treasured hot months are the only time anyone should see your feet outside the bedroom.

Hand Signals

What to do with your hands when you're dressed for business

To look as if you actually belong in your top-of-the-line suit, it's not sufficient just to buy the suit and put it on with care. Those are mere levels one and two. To sell yourself convincingly in an expensive suit, you need to know what to do with your body, particularly your hands, when you're in it. It's the secret to looking great in fine tailoring. And so we present you with three easy moves to try at your next social occasion. Each of them will have you looking as if you're wearing the suit instead of the other way around.

THE PRINCE CHARLES

The Move: Absentminded fiddling with the cuff links.
The Purpose: To ensure that precisely one inch of your shirt's cuff is showing at all times. The bonus: With your arms balanced, your suit's fitted shape is emphasized. You'll look royal. When it's done: Transitional movements—between the limo and the official reception, in elevators, or arriving at parties.
Pitfall: Do not attempt this if your shirt does not have French cuffs. You'll just look nervous.

THE BONAPARTE

The Move: One hand slipped flat into the opening of your suit.
The Purpose: To conceal shaky hands or delirium tremens. The bonus: You'll be quick on the draw if there's a need for a tip. When it's done: Oaths of allegiance, photo ops, award speeches, greeting lines.
Pitfalls: Never grasp or palm your breast. Just keep your hand flat and relaxed. And never attempt to "Bonaparte" other people, particularly women.

THE UPPER EAST THUMB

The Move: One hand sitting in the side jacket pocket with your thumb jutting forward.
The Purpose: To appear at ease even in stuffy surroundings. The bonus: The crook of your arm away from your body emphasizes slimness. When it's done: At yacht clubs, ritzy East Coast cocktail parties that *Esquire* is no longer invited to.
Pitfalls: Do not put undue weight on your pocket edge. The hand should float while inside the pocket. Also, never do this with both hands at once. Symmetry is a no-no.

{ *The RULES* }
•
JACKET SLEEVES ARE TAILORED SO THAT HALF AN INCH OF SHIRT CUFF SHOWS WHEN YOUR ARMS ARE AT YOUR SIDES. This does not make your sleeves look shorter. It makes your arms look longer. Work it out.

THE ANATOMY OF

The Tuxedo

Men are returning to the notion of being properly attired for the event at hand—which means no more cutting corners on your evening wear. You don't need all the bells and whistles, but you do need a tux and a handful of the right accessories.

1. THE SHIRT
White piqué cotton, bib-front or with vertical razor pleats, pressed until it's immaculate. French cuffs are essential. Try to find a fine lightweight cotton for comfort. A turndown collar is more comfortable; a wing collar is more dressy.

2. THE TUX
Peaked lapels, single- or double-breasted. Notch lapels make you look like a waiter. Black wool barathea is classic, but a lighter plain weave is better for summer comfort. Grosgrain lapels last longer; satin has a habit of snagging and showing its age quicker. Midnight blue is very cool.

3. THE BOW TIE
Silk satin or silk grosgrain, black. Adjustable versions make tying easier, but you should tie it yourself.

4. THE POCKET SQUARE
In cotton or linen, not silk, which will slip.

5. THE CUMMERBUND
The cummerbund (from the Hindi for "waistband"), anachronistic or not, is still essential. Without it, you look as if you're not trying.

6. THE SHOES
You do not need patent-leather shoes, although they look sharp. A good pair of well-polished cap-toe oxfords will suffice.

DECIPHERING THE DRESS CODE

The Invitation Translator

WHAT IT SAYS	WHAT IT IMPLIES	WHAT IT REALLY MEANS
Black tie	Tuxedo only, and not a black suit	*Tuxedo only, and not a black suit*
Cocktail attire	A suit, shirt, and tie	*Don't look as if you came straight from the office, even if you did*
Black-tie optional	You can choose between black tie and a suit	*Black tie*
Alternative black tie	Black tie, but with a twist	*Black tie*
Business casual	Polo shirt, chinos	*A dress shirt that's not a polo shirt. No sneakers, no jeans.*
Come as you are	Take a shower, at least	*Dress any way you like*
P.B.A.B.	Please bring a bottle— of wine	*Bring a bottle of good wine*

The "in-between" suit—straddling the work suit and the tuxedo—is a specialized breed. It should have narrower-than-normal lapels for a crisper silhouette (the outline of the suit), and the fabric should have a slight sheen to it. • Spend a little extra on the shirt. The shirt should complement the suit—and not just in terms of color. The narrow lapels of the jacket demand a narrow-collared shirt. Got wide lapels? Wear a bold spread collar that can stand up to them. • The tie can make a statement, including "Work's over—I've taken mine off." If you go without neckwear, though, don't skip the pocket square—one with a little color in it.

HOW TO WEAR THE "IN-BETWEEN" SUIT

Actually, consider the pocket square your life vest. It's the early twenty-first century version of neckwear. • Alternative dressing up does not apply to the feet, an area whose dignity must not be toyed with. Shoes should be something interesting— which is different from flamboyant. Classic brown wing tips don't beg for attention; they simply draw it to themselves. • Black-tie events are not, unless you are in a band, acceptable moments to dress up alternatively. • The higher the visible quality of the fabric, the more casually it can be worn. • A fancy watch on your wrist never hurts.

THE RAT PACK AND THE TUXEDO

➡ *In the early 1960s, the Rat Pack, the legendary show-biz trinity of Frank Sinatra, Dean Martin, and Sammy Davis Jr., personified swinger cool—a life of jazz-and-cocktails that somehow left them looking freshly pressed and impeccably groomed. A large part of that raffish-but-manicured mystique belongs to the tuxedo, the Pack's sharply tailored working uniform. James Bond's Agent 007, another of the era's world-class rakes, was a fellow poster boy for the tuxedo's aura of effortless swank.*

THE ESSENTIAL RULES OF

Black Tie

Wearing a tuxedo can be a lot like speaking an unfamiliar language. The smallest mistake can ruin the whole effect. Here's how to get it right.

- You can add personal touches after you've nailed the standard. For your basic tux, stick with tradition. This dictates a one-button jacket with peaked lapels, a true pleat-front or marcella-front shirt (with French cuffs), black wool or silk socks, and black patent-leather lace-ups or polished oxfords. Bow tie only, in red or black (and tied yourself—it's the mark of a gentleman). And a cummerbund, of course.

- The pleats of the cummerbund should face upward.

- Your cuff links should match your watch: gold with gold, silver with steel, and so on.

- Leave your wallet at home and take a money clip instead. It's smaller, so it won't distort the lines of your tux.

Frequently Asked Questions

The Tuxedo

Q **How do I buy a tuxedo that will be fashionable now and in thirty years?**
Try a one- or two-button tux in a wool-mohair blend, perhaps in a hopsack weave—the salesperson will understand—with grosgrain lapels, not satin, which is more fragile and shows its age more easily. Choose peaked, not notched, lapels, which are less susceptible to the whims of fashion than a shawl collar. Go for single-pleat pants with waistband side tabs for a bit of size adaptability. Dry-clean no more than once a year; dry cleaning will do more damage to your tux than wearing it will. Keep it in a hanging suit bag on a properly shaped wood hanger when not in use.

{ The RULES }
•
WAITERS WHO SIT AT YOUR TABLE *when they take your order usually get it wrong.*

How Not to Look Like a Waiter
•

NO NOTCHED LAPELS–PEAKED OR SHAWL LAPELS ONLY.
ONE-BUTTON JACKET, NOT THREE-BUTTON. WEAR A PROPER EVENING SHIRT.
WEAR A CUMMERBUND. TIE YOUR OWN TIE, AND STOP FILLING OTHER PEOPLE'S GLASSES.

Signs your
SUIT DOESN'T FIT

The jacket's shoulder pads are supposed to sit on your shoulder. If they droop off and leave dents in the cloth, the jacket's too big. Go down a size.

The jacket's sleeves should never reach farther than the point where the base of the thumb meets the wrist. If they do, go down a size.

You do not need enough room in your jacket to house a family of raccoons. Go down two sizes.

Pants should touch the shoes with only an inch of cloth to spare. Anything more should be taken up.

HOW to BUY a BUSINESS SUIT

1. Prioritize.

The basic unit of workplace style is the navy blue suit. It should be your first purchase. After that comes solid charcoal gray. Then striped and checked versions of these two fundamental shades. The black suit is tempting but should be resisted: Hit men and undertakers are not a businessman's role models.

2. Spend. Wisely.

The right $1,200 suit, fitted by a tailor, is better than two $800 suits off the rack.

3. Mitigate headaches.

Sure, the weightless vicuña blends and the fine-as-silk Super 180's look good. But they're also a pain to take care of. All-season mid-weight cloths feel good summer through winter, and resilient weaves like hopsack and gabardine won't wrinkle on a red-eye.

4. Maximize utility.

Chosen carefully, the three basic suits–one navy, one gray, and a pattern–can constitute an entire wardrobe. A dozen shirts and ties, in different colors and fabrics, turn them into a limitless backdrop for creativity.

5. Check the fit.

Most American men were never trained to know what a perfectly fitted suit means—high armholes, a slight silhouette at the torso, nothing too baggy at the crotch. You owe it to yourself to discover and revel in the power of a perfect fit. *SEE OPPOSITE* ❍

THE TROUSER BOTTOM

Only a little cloth should ever drape on your shoes; ask your tailor for a one-inch break in your front crease. The hem of your pants should cover the laces of your shoes and slope slightly downward toward the heel, stopping about an inch above the welt. The front crease of your trouser leg should "break" slightly at mid-shin. If the crease is dead straight, your pants are too short.

THE SHOULDER AND THE LAPEL

How your jacket fits at the shoulder is the first sign of whether a man knows his size. Look for higher, smaller armholes and a narrower sleeve. It fits properly if there's no overhang at the shoulder pad or, conversely, your shoulder does not bulge out at the top of the sleeve. A smooth curving line should fall from sleeve head to cuff. No outline of your own shoulder should appear in the sleeve, and the sleeve's head should never sag.

THE WAIST

The correct waist measurement is not at your hips, as you've been trained to believe. Nor is it at your belly button, as women have been trained to believe. It's halfway in between. While your correct waist measurement may cause initial shock, knowing it will make your suit fit better.

There should be no creases or ripples radiating from the single fastened button. If there are, switch up a size (or, even better, lose some weight).

THE SHIRT CUFF

A quarter to a half inch of shirt cuff should always be visible. Maintaining this is one of life's greatest challenges. And the sleeve should rest a half inch below your wristbone.

THE COLLAR

The collar of your jacket should sit well on the shoulders and not buckle or pucker, stand away from or conceal your shirt collar. One half-inch of shirt collar should be visible at the back.

THE JACKET LENGTH

The bottom hem should be level with your knuckles. (Or, alternatively, it should be just long enough to cover your rear.)

WHICH SHAPE ARE YOU?

There's a suit to fit each one

Are you a "drop six"? If you are, you're a suit maker's dream: Your chest is six inches larger than your waist. You can wear anything. Sadly, most of us don't live inside those ideal tailoring measurements. Instead, in pursuit of comfort, most red-blooded American men leave the department store with a suit that's a size too big or just plain not right for their body type. So what do you do if you're not a suit maker's dream shape? Skip the expensive custom tailor and follow this cheat sheet.

Your shape: **SQUARE**	Your shape: **THE INVERTED V**	Your shape: **THE BEANPOLE**	Your shape: **THE ATHLETIC V**
A square man's jacket should be just long enough to cover his rear end but not cut too much on the long side; that only shortens those efficient legs. Go for a two-button with a double vent, which gives the illusion of longer legs. Angle for dark, striped cloths, with no wide shoulders or lapels.	Sporting your seasonal gut? No problem. One- and two-button jackets with a deep gorge, or opening, will elongate the body. Narrow pinstripes and chalk stripes also do the trick. Balance your respectable waistline with strong shoulders and wider lapels.	Create breadth by adopting the three-button suit (with a higher button closure). Draw attention to the chest and neck by way of brighter hues and patterns on your neckties and shirts. Do not be tempted to widen yourself with excess padding, though; you'll just look that much skinnier.	A two-button suit gives a deeper gorge and allows room for bigger biceps. Look for larger armholes and wider sleeves. Your guns should not be visible through cloth. Found the ideal jacket but the pants are too big? Grease the salesman into switching out the pants for a smaller suit.

THE RIGHT SUIT AMPLIFIES YOUR PHYSICAL STRENGTHS AND DIMINISHES YOUR SHORTCOMINGS

•

A large man should wear solids, especially dark ones, and avoid large, loud patterns. A short man elongates his silhouette with a suit, particularly a striped suit, eschewing the sport-coat-and-pants look because it chops in half what little verticality he has. And ye of the ample booty: Go with ventless jackets or those with a rear vent rather than side-vented models, which flap above your prodigious glutes like a signal flag.

How to Buy for Your Body Type

You are	You want	Avoid
BIG & TALL (e.g., Andre the Giant)	*Pants with cuffs to break up your seemingly endless inseam; pants with slimming, shallow pleats; a dark navy suit.*	*Anything with horizontal lines, which accentuate your girth; anything with vertical lines, which make you look taller.*
LONG & LEAN (e.g., Barack Obama)	*Anything with horizontal lines to help you look broader; three-button jackets that match the scale of your torso.*	*Anything with vertical lines, which only make you look taller; tight suits and jackets that advertise your thin limbs.*
SHORT & STOCKY (e.g., Danny DeVito)	*Single-button suits that have a deep V at the chest to make the torso look longer; V-neck sweaters that do the same.*	*Anything with horizontal stripes or busy plaids, which break up the body's vertical lines; wide pants and cuffs.*
SHORT & LEAN (e.g., Tom Cruise)	*Two-button suit jackets that work in proportion to your torso; thicker fabrics (like corduroy), which offer the illusion of heft.*	*Anything baggy or loose, which draws attention to your size; anything that's all black.*

Why It's Made the Way It's Made

Why should I have working buttons on my sleeve?
Because otherwise it's like getting a Mercedes without power windows. If you're going to get a great suit, then you pay the extra eighty-five dollars for buttonholes. Trust us. Hand-sewn buttonholes are still a sign of a good suit, but be aware that even cheap suits have mock buttonholes, sewn by machine.

My suits always seem to form a bump at the back of my neck. Is this normal?
Normal, no. Common, yes. The bump happens when there's too much fabric above the shoulder line, causing it to pucker. A tailor should be able to fix this, because nowhere on your suit should

there appear anything that might be called a pucker. Yes, even if the suit was on sale. The jacket should hug your neck gently and rest cleanly and comfortably on your shoulders. No bumps.

Why is an unlined suit more expensive than a lined one?
When there's no lining, any visible seams must be perfectly finished; there's no room for error. It's painstaking and costly, but the jacket will be softer and cooler. Our choice is the partially lined jacket (like the one turned inside-out, above); pieces of viscose cloth sewn in strategic places make it easy to slide the jacket on and off without compromising the cool fabric.

Do I need shoulder padding in my suit?
Personal preference. Suits generally have either a soft shoulder (fabric only) or a structured one (varying amounts of padding). Either is appropriate, but the soft shoulder is cooler, looks more casual, and allows the fabric to drape more naturally. The structured shoulder, slightly padded, will look more crisp and add to your stature. Beware, though, of too much padding, which will make you look like Bea Arthur.

{ The RULES }

•

THERE IS NO ALTERING OF SHOULDERS.
If the jacket doesn't fit there, it never will.

THE HIDDEN DETAIL

Fused vs. Canvased

INSIDE EVERY PROPER suit jacket, between the exterior cloth and the lining, lies the secret of its shape: a layer of cloth called the canvas. A bespoke suit or a top-end ready-to-wear design features what's known as a full-hand canvas, sewn into the jacket by hand, stitch by stitch, so that it echoes the curves of the chest, gives the lapel its roll, and, in a sense, determines the very integrity of the jacket. Cheaper brands, however, use a process called fusing, in which a synthetic interlining is heated by machine until it adheres to the exterior fabric and provides the jacket with its rudimentary shape. Until you're caught in a rainstorm, that is, when the glue dissolves, leaving blisters on the chest and lapels. Although fusing has long been deemed inferior to hand canvasing, this is no longer universally so. Improvements in fusing technology have made it possible to create fused suits that fit better than some canvased ones. Never, however, offer this opinion to a tailor, unless he be of robust constitution.

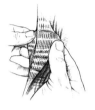

How to Tell
Pinch an inch of the jacket's fabric, preferably between the bottom two buttonholes. If you feel only two layers, that means the jacket is fused: You will feel only the exterior and the inner facing. If you feel three layers, that means the jacket is canvased, and what you're sensing is the facing, the exterior, and the canvas itself floating in between. If after performing this test, you're still not sure, ask the salesman. If he doesn't know what you're talking about, you're probably in the wrong store.

SUIT SEAMS
Hand-sewn vs. machine-sewn

Hand-sewn seams are composed of a single thread running through the fabric in a wavelike pattern. When done properly, they are smooth and pucker-free and are more resilient to creasing and stretching than machined seams.

Machine-sewn seams are composed of two threads looped tightly around each other in a chainlike pattern. They are sturdy, but the loops create puckers in the fabric, which can worsen over time as the fabric stretches.

RULES FOR BUYING A SUIT

•

There's a reason it's on sale. **When in doubt, go with the two-button.** *Beware the salesman who works on commission.* **No two suit brands are cut the same way. So if you don't get a good fit from one brand, try a different one.** *Listen to your tailor, but always follow your gut.* **Re: Your gut—a good tailor can help you with that.** *The more elaborate the pattern, the less often you'll wear it.* **Assuming you won't set off alarms, take your prospective purchase outside and look at it in daylight. Hidden depths and colors may appear.** *Most reputable shops offer on-site tailoring services. Take advantage of them.* **Anyone who orders a suit online deserves exactly what's coming to him.** *A three-piece suit says you mean business; in fact, it says you mean to take over the business.*

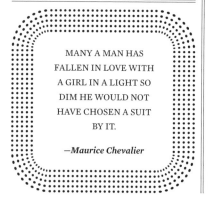

MANY A MAN HAS FALLEN IN LOVE WITH A GIRL IN A LIGHT SO DIM HE WOULD NOT HAVE CHOSEN A SUIT BY IT.

—*Maurice Chevalier*

What to expect when you buy a custom-made suit

THE BESPOKE LIFE

A bespoke suit can be a man's greatest gift to himself, and the term *bespoke* even has its origins on Savile Row. (When a customer chose a bolt of fabric for his suit, that fabric would then "be spoken for.") Yet the sheer scope of options, from cloth and cut to lapels and lining, can be daunting. How do you avoid a minor existential crisis?

FIRST, FIND A GOOD TAILOR. The best way is to ask a man you trust; if a suit maker has the respect of your peers, he probably deserves it.

THE INFINITE VARIETY: A good tailor will guide you through the maze of choices with your wits intact. And a clever tailor will always advise that your first suit remain free of any showy details (the better to appreciate the fit and quality of work.)

THE PROCESS: The tailor will take up to twenty-five measurements before sending you on your way. You'll return for the first fitting, when every square inch of the embryonic suit is evaluated and adjusted. The suit will go through two or three further cycles over several months. Finally, slip on the finished product and smile.

WAIT TIME: Six weeks to a year
COST: In the $3,000 range
NUMBER OF FITTINGS: At least three to four.

HOW TO

Keep a Suit Forever

HOW TO

STORE A SUIT

OUT OF SEASON

Fully sealed in a suit-length or hanging Space Bag (see p. 212) with the air removed by a vacuum cleaner. Hang on a well-shaped hanger. Dry-clean suit first to ensure against moth damage. Take time to lay it flat (to reduce creases before vacuuming out the air).

THE BRISTLED CLEANING DEVICE
Your grandfather used a suit brush. He was a wise man. Far from being a pointless tool in the age of dry cleaning, the clothes brush (along with steaming) allows you to put off dry cleaning. Before brushing, air out your suit near an open window, then lay it flat on the table.

THE RAIN DEFLECTOR
These days even high-end designers use cheaper and less-labor-intensive fused linings to give jackets the structure they need. When your suit jacket gets wet, it puckers and becomes misshapen. No amount of pressing can bring a suit back from this condition.

IN SEASON

On a generously shaped hanger in a zipped-up suit bag.

THE GARMENT-SUSPENSION DEVICE
Every time you don't store your jacket on one of these (it's a hanger, by the way), you're cutting its life. Look for the same qualities in hangers as you do in your best pirate friends: a generous thickness to the shoulder and a strong metal hook. A suit hanger should be broad and shaped enough to support a jacket much the way it might hang on you. Anything less and it risks looking like it has just been slept in.

THE STEAM-DELIVERY TOOL
You need to dry-clean a suit only once a year. Any more and the process can weaken it and ruin its shape. Steaming is the ideal solution for keeping the suit looking immaculate. (Steaming a suit while actually wearing it is not ideal at all. But it is amusing.)

{ *The RULES* }

•

THINGS YOU SHOULD NOT HANG YOUR SUIT JACKET OR BLAZER ON:
The back of a chair, a bed post, a wire hanger, bare skin (unless it's a woman's), the exacta at the Kentucky Derby.

•

PLACES WHERE YOU SHOULD NOT WEAR A SUIT: The beach (unless you're getting married on one), the rodeo, a monster truck rally.

The **SARTORIAL CANON**

>>> • <<<

The Suit

BRIONI	➤ Named for a resort island in the Adriatic, this Italian suit maker was founded in Rome in 1945. Its sleekly cut, hand-sewn garments belong to the Roman sartorial tradition, more fitted and structured than the softer Neapolitan look. Brioni power suits hang on the shoulders of Kofi Annan, Donald Trump, James Bond, and an international roster of VIPs. www.brioni.com
BROOKS BROTHERS	➤ Opened in 1818, Brooks Brothers has done much more than invent the classic American sack suit back in 1895. Its other sartorial innovations include the ready-to-wear suit (1845), and the two-button suit (1961). Beyond its Ivy League staples, Brooks Brothers offers well-made, reasonably priced tailored clothing and a more contemporary line, Black Fleece, by designer Thom Browne. www.brooksbrothers.com
CANALI	➤ Founded in 1934 by two brothers and still family owned and run, Canali produces some of Italy's finest high-end ready-to-wear suits. Canali's suave suits are made and hand-finished entirely in Italy, an increasingly rare practice. www.canali.it
GIEVES & HAWKES	➤ Located at No. 1 Savile Row since 1912, tailor Gieves & Hawkes was formed by the merger of two older English houses. The firm produced the Row's first ready-to-wear suits in 1922. Today the London store still offers traditional bespoke services, but the company also produces internationally distributed collections that give a modern spin to classic English style. www.gievesandhawkes.com
HICKEY FREEMAN	➤ Founded a century ago in Rochester, New York, Hickey Freeman was among the first clothing manufacturers to use modern assembly-line techniques. It still makes handsome, classic, conservative American suits in the factory it opened in 1915. The company recently launched a youth-focused brand, Hickey, that offers slim-fitting suits and casual wear. www.hickeyfreeman.com

•

CHAPTER TWO

The Shirt
AND THE
Sweater

....

WEARING A SHIRT AND TIE MAY GET OLD,
*but thanks in part to the First World War,
at least the collar of your favorite dress shirt
doesn't threaten your jugular, and there's no need to
rummage in your drawers each morning for a
requisite cravat pin and watch fob.* ➥

....

THROUGHOUT MUCH of the nineteenth century and the Edwardian era leading up to the war, traditional dress shirts had detachable white linen collars, starched rigid and worn high. A writer for *The Gentlemen's Journal* complained in a 1909 article about "the curious, stiff, high, turn-over, close-locking collars which I see in hotel corridors and streets. How hideous they are." Right. We've all been there, man.

THE DEMOBILIZED SERVICEMEN returning home from the Great War were apparently also in no mood for restrictive civilian clothes. In the manner of impetuous young people everywhere—whether the Lost Generation or Generation X, Y, or Z—gentlemen of the Jazz Age embraced change. Their sartorial rebellion was expressed in the form of fine shirts that draped naturally over the body, with soft collars that folded back from the neck. F. Scott Fitzgerald paid homage to the new style in *The Great Gatsby*, when Daisy Buchanan famously buries her face in a pile of Jay Gatsby's luscious-hued English shirts and sobs uncontrollably at their overwhelming beauty.

MEN EVER SINCE have enjoyed choosing from an astonishing array of style options. Roaring Twenties collar styles, including the button-down, the tab, the pinned, and the Barrymore (a long-point number named for the matinee idol), have continued to go in and out of fashion. The Windsor, an extreme spread style designed to accommodate the hefty tie knots favored by the eponymous Duke, made its debut in the 1930s. It's still the dressiest of dress-shirt collars, sported by corporate moguls and deposed royals; beyond it, you're in tuxedo territory—the only social situation in which you're still obliged to wear a white shirt.

AND WHAT, YOU MAY ASK, is there to say about this minimalist wardrobe staple? For starters, there is no dressy occasion when wearing a white dress shirt is a style faux pas. It always looks good, provided it's clean, it fits you, has all its buttons intact, and has met an iron at some point in its recent history. True, it can seem an unadventurous choice, particularly with a business suit, but there is no shame in embodying a fine tradition. Worn with jeans and a sport jacket, a crisp white shirt is as dashing a statement as ever.

THE SPORT SHIRT—an open-collar, short-sleeve, button-front style in woven or knitted fabrics—first showed up in the 1930s, too, mostly at exclusive winter watering holes like Monte Carlo and Palm Beach, since only the rich needed smart leisure clothes during the Depression. The new shirts, first made of light cottons and linens, were intended to be worn without a tie but still look casually elegant. Their twenty-first-century descendents have a slightly vintage feel that captures the timeless cool of the postwar era. Think Palm Springs and Cary Grant circa 1959; beware of Waikiki Beach and Don Ho circa 1977. The watchword is bold, never garish.

NOT ALL THE SPORT shirt's progeny are so pedigreed. That great social leveler, the T-shirt, started life as humble underwear but, made of tissue-weight cashmere or silk, can now carry a three-figure price tag. Somewhere in between lies the perfect T: high-quality, 100 percent cotton, black or white, true to its American roots. Worn with a well-cut pair of khakis, a belt, and polished loafers, it will take you pretty much anywhere except to the office.

THE WOOL SWEATER has proved even more universally popular. Originally the garb of laborers, farm workers, and fishermen, it was adopted enthusiastically by Jazz Age urbanites, for whom slipping on a stretchy pullover had the same liberating charge as throwing out starched collars and shirts. In England, the actor and playwright Noël Coward, fed up with collars and ties, began wearing colored turtlenecks, "actually more for comfort than for effect," he said. "Soon I was informed by my evening paper that I had started a fashion." No generation since has been willing to give up the comfort and ease of the sweater, and for our money, there's no more comfortable and better-looking option than a merino wool or cashmere V-neck worn with a tie and sport jacket or suit. Because it comes in myriad guises—including contemporary zip-fronts and bold colors—changing your style can be as simple as slipping on a different pullover.

The DRESS SHIRT

Everything you need to know to build the perfect shirt wardrobe

➤ THE BOTTOM BUTTON

On the well-made dress shirt, the buttonholes are all cut and sewn vertically into the placket, except for the very bottom one, which is horizontal. This is because shirts used to button into the front of the trousers to prevent blousing, and even though pants no longer accommodate this, the finest shirtmakers have clung to the tradition.

➤ THE BOX PLEAT

A nice detail on the dress shirt is the box pleat, which drops from the yoke (the piece of fabric that goes over the shoulder) to the bottom of the shirt and provides greater roominess in the shirt's back.

➤ THE HAND-SEWN SHOULDER

Only on a very high quality (read: expensive) dress shirt will the sleeve be hand-sewn to the yoke with the stripes of each piece lining up perfectly.

➤ THE CONTRASTING COLLAR

Created so that white-collar types could wear colorful shirts without losing status, the contrast collar is now a favorite with dandies. Shown is a collar cut on the bias to withstand many washings without shrinking.

➤ THE PLACKET

The place where the buttonholes run down the front of your shirt is called the placket. On a well-made dress shirt, the placket is a separate piece of material (left), sewn on with a single-needle machine. Alternately, in super-lightweight summer dress shirts, there may be no placket at all (right), in order to keep the shirt cool and elegant.

➤ THE GUSSET

A gusset is added for reinforcement at the bottom of the shirt where the front and back join.

➤ THE BUTTONS

Mother-of-pearl buttons are a sign of a well-made shirt. The thicker the better, to withstand washings; four holes mean a better bind.

EVERY MAN NEEDS A
White Dress Shirt

On the totem pole of necessity, a white dress shirt sits somewhere between a belt and a toothbrush. Can you imagine not owning one? But merely owning any white dress shirt is not enough. The perfect specimen must:

- Fit exquisitely
- Have thick buttons (preferably mother-of-pearl)
- Be constructed of fine cotton
- Be of impeccable quality (the simplicity of the shirt will reveal any imperfections)

Wear your perfect white dress shirt with something striking—like a dark suit and tie and a white pocket square—and everyone notices. *Everyone*. The word women use is sharp. Or dapper. Or fantastic. They often touch your shoulder or lay their hand on your forearm. Men tell you you look "great," and they say it with something like puzzlement or suspicion. The look is nothing new. But worn right, it works like a charm.

YOUR COLLAR SHOULD COMPLEMENT YOUR FACE.

Round face? Point collar.
Narrow face? Spread collar.
Cris Collinsworth?
With a neck that long, the highest-sitting collar money can buy.

{ *The* CLASSICS }
The Brooks Brothers Button-Down

FAVORED BY SUCH UNCONVENTIONAL style icons as Andy Warhol and Gianni Agnelli, the term *button-down* is often misused by fashion rookies to describe a shirt that has buttons down the center from top to bottom. No. The term button-down actually refers to having the ends of the shirt collar fastened to the shirt by buttons. John Brooks, grandson of the founder of America's most venerable clothing brand, did not invent the button-down shirt, but he made it a pillar of American style. At a polo match in England in 1896, Brooks noticed that players had added buttons to their shirt collars to keep them from flapping while riding. He immediately adopted the technique. Seeing its usefulness, he brought the practice to America and began selling the classic button-down dress shirt in 1900. It defined America's knack for a more casual, functional approach to dressing well, and by the 1920s it was an American staple. The button-down has survived in fashionable and square wardrobes alike, despite its conservative connotations.

**ANDY WARHOL AND
THE DRESS SHIRT**
➥ *"Why do people think
artists are so special?" Andy
Warhol once quipped. "It's
just another job." Warhol felt
art was a business just like
any other. As if to prove
the point, he often wore
components of a business-
man's uniform—a dress shirt
and necktie—straight up and
without irony. His ensemble
meant exactly what it
implied: I'm a commercial
artist; what of it? If surface
truth was the only kind
Warhol believed in, he wore
the truth on his sleeve.*

The Dress Shirt

Q *Can one wear a blue shirt with a white collar, often called a banker's shirt, without a tie?*
No—unless you're Oliver Barrett IV, walking around your Ivy League campus in your grandpa's clothes and hitting on the Italian girl at the library. Otherwise, wear the tie. Most men who wear the contrasting collar are interested neither in comfort nor in expressing their individuality. If you're trying to break free of your own gray-flannel prison, try something that's meant to be dressed down, like a sweatshirt.

When do I need to tuck in my shirt?
Q For some, the only answer to this question is "always." For others, a few kinds of shirts can be worn untucked with impunity. These include a casual shirt with a bottom hem that cuts straight across and doesn't hang below the hipbone, anything knitted (e.g., polo shirts), and, of course, fitted T-shirts. For the rest of your shirts, tuck them in, and don't even think about doing that half-tucked, one-side-in-one-side-out business. That only works if you're twenty-four and dating an actress, and even then it doesn't look good.

A FIELD GUIDE to the SHIRT

THE CUFF

1. THE ONE-BUTTON BARREL. Here's your basic anywhere, anytime cuff. Functional and modern, with none of the fiddliness of cuff links, the one-button cuff is right for normal office days but not too dressy.

2. TWO-BUTTON NOTCHED BARREL. A nice detail that, for formality, is just short of French. The notch and slightly longer cuff upgrade an everyday suit and can dress up a sport coat worn with trousers or jeans.

THE COLLAR

1. THE BUTTON-DOWN. *The least formal of the collar styles, it should be worn with nothing dressier than a sport coat. And always buttoned.*

2. THE MEDIUM SPREAD. *A handsome option appropriate with almost any suit and face shape, and with a variety of tie knots.*

> **{ The RULES }**
> •
> **ONCE THE COLLAR OF A WHITE DRESS SHIRT YELLOWS**, *it's time to get a new white dress shirt.*

3. THE TWO-BUTTON TURNBACK.

A smart look that skews to the dandy. Rare but in the ascendant, the turnback cuff was popularized by the first James Bond, Sean Connery, in *Dr. No*. It combines the elegance of a double cuff with the ease of buttons.

4. THE FRENCH.

Still the most dressed-up choice, the double, or French cuff, is best for showing a quarter inch of shirt cuff from underneath your jacket sleeve. With a simple silk knot or a plain silver cuff link, it shows them that you know exactly what you're doing.

3. THE TWO-BUTTON SPREAD.

Set on a wider band with two buttons at the neck, the tall collar can be worn without a tie altogether, since it's substantial enough on its own. Sits nice and high on the neck, so it works well for the tall, wiry guy who needs some height to cover the neck. Its tie knot: the half Windsor.

4. THE STRAIGHT-POINT.

A classic shape that works for all ages and neck shapes. Good for the round-faced or short-necked man, as it neither accentuates girth nor hides the neck. Its tie knot: the Windsor, or anything suitably chunky. Don't forget the collar stays.

THE FABRIC

You know there's a whole range of weaves, even before color plays into it. But did you know that certain weaves beg pairing with certain ties? Now you do. There are many options, so herewith, some of the most popular.

1. Sea-island cotton. This very light, almost translucent woven cotton works best with silks and other lightweights.

2. Diagonal-weave brushed twill. A textured cotton with a fine pattern, this meaty weave can carry off the chunkiest of woven silk ties.

3. End-on-end broadcloth. Combines white with another color cotton in a very fine weave that results in a tiny check. May be paired with sturdy fabrics like thick silk wovens.

4. Pima. This lightweight, supersoft option coordinates with lightweight silk, cotton, and linen ties.

The Rules of Wearing Shirts

How tight to knot your tie, when your shirt collar is just right,
where to put a monogram, and more

TIP AT THE WAIST	DIMPLE IN THE MIDDLE	TIE IT TIGHT
The point should just touch the waistband of your suit trousers, assuming, of course, that your waistband is properly on or just above your hipbone.	Just one dimple. In the middle, secured with a pinch. Edges that are curled forward are sloppy. Practice until it's right.	When tied, the knot should sit high under the collar, so that practically no material can be seen above the knot between the collar edges.

THE TIE CLIP	KNOW YOUR NECK SIZE	STICK LETTERS HERE

Designed to keep your tie in place, the tie clip should slide in from the wearer's right to grip both the tie and the placket of your shirt around the middle of the sternum.	The collar fits when you can just slip your index and middle fingers side by side snugly between your collar and neck. Any tighter and you risk discomfort.	Place a monogram anywhere you like. The most classic location is directly below the middle of the breast pocket. Visible but not obtrusive.

AN OVERSIMPLIFIED GUIDE TO
Mixing Patterns

*How to pair shirts and ties
without incident or injury.*

1. FINE-STRIPED SHIRT
Best bet: A textured
knit tie.

2. CHECKERED SHIRT
Best bet: A dark solid
tie with a subtle pattern.

3. WINDOWPANE SHIRT
Best bet: A patterned
tie that echoes the
color of the check.

4. GLEN-PLAID SHIRT
Best bet: A thick-
striped tie that accents
the bolder plaid.

5. WOVEN SHIRT
Best bet: A dark tie
with stripes that match
the shirt.

**6. BENGAL-STRIPED
SHIRT**
Best bet: A dark solid tie
with a subtle pattern.

***GORDON GEKKO AND
THE BANKER'S SHIRT***
➤ *Michael Douglas as
Gordon Gekko, poster boy
for bankers gone wild in
the 1987 film* Wall Street, *accessorized the plunderer
look impeccably: loosened
silk tie, striped suspenders,
slicked-back hair, and cobra-like stare.* Wall Street *didn't
invent the contrast-collar
shirt, which has been around
at least since Edwardian
times, but the colored shirt
and white spread collar
became notorious during
the Reagan era, when the
most rapacious businessmen
adopted it as battle dress for
high-testosterone takeovers.*

SIX SHIRTS AND TIES
RULES FOR WEARING 'EM

If there is one consistent expression of a man's sartorial acumen, it's the way in which he pairs his shirt with his tie. Daily, we are forced to witness new transgressions in the coordination of upper-body adornment by grown men. You dress yourselves in such a manner as to inspire women to cover their children's eyes and say silent prayers. It's not that hard. It's all trial and error and requires only an eye for color. If you don't have one, do not improvise. Ask the salesman. It's his job. And take a cue from what you see on your well-turned-out peers, or the guys in ads, or the combos below. Do it for the children. And while the art of matching the two is always up to the individual, there are still some rules. Here, three to remember:

Bold graphic statements such as matching a red tie with a plain white shirt or sporting a contrasting collar will convey the power of a Donald Trump or a Gordon Gekko.

To go with the new breed of lean-cut suits, you should ditch the plain oxford in favor of a striped shirt paired with a narrow tie.

And don't forget, the pattern on your tie should never be more noticeable than the one on your shirt.

THE USEFUL PART:
ANIMALS MAKE THE BEST LOGOS

POLO

LACOSTE

BROOKS BROTHERS

PENGUIN

{ *The* CLASSICS }
The Polo Shirt

Inspired by the wool-knit jerseys worn by polo players since the 1890s, René Lacoste appeared at the 1926 US Open in a short-sleeved, soft-collared, white cotton pullover. Custom-made polo shirts were soon indispensable sportswear items for members of the leisure class on both sides of the Atlantic. In 1933, Lacoste and the French knitwear manufacturer André Gillier began marketing cotton piqué shirts embossed with the now-familiar alligator logo—a branding innovation that launched an ark's worth of miniature animals nestled on sporting chests. Lacoste's alligator, introduced to the American market in 1952, was joined by Munsingwear's penguin in 1955 and Ralph Lauren's polo player and pony in 1972. A casual wear perennial that, like blue jeans, can be dressed up or down, the polo shirt became something of a fashion item in the prep-obsessed early 1980s (never mind that fuchsia pink and flipped-up collars might not have been what the estimable M. Lacoste had in mind). The polo periodically enjoys a style renaissance among young trendsetters—of late, among those eschewing scrappy vintage T-shirts for a snappier appearance.

RENÉ LACOSTE AND THE POLO SHIRT

➤ *Legendary French tennis champ René Lacoste didn't pick up a racket until he was fifteen, but his tenacity on the court earned him the nickname Le Crocodile. His determination extended to his attire: In 1926, he debuted the white polo shirt on court, disregarding the regulation dress code that included a long-sleeved, stiff-collared shirt, tie, and long white flannel pants. Half a century later, the chameleonic polo lent ironic cool to art-rock superstars like David Byrne of Talking Heads, who often wore one onstage.*

STEVE McQUEEN AND THE BLACK TURTLENECK

➡ *In 1968 tight-lipped actor Steve McQueen, playing a San Francisco cop in* Bullitt, *gave the black turtleneck—a symbol of the beatnik rebellion in the 1950s—a shot of tough-guy charisma. (The double holster also helped.) In its heyday from the 1950s through the 1970s, the turtleneck was seen on cool culture cats from Dizzy Gillespie to McQueen and Michael Caine, shown here playing a spy with quiet confidence in* The Eagle Has Landed *in 1976.*

{ *The* CLASSICS }
The Cable-Knit Sweater

FIRST EMERGING AS a wardrobe staple in the United States during the 1950s, the cable-knit became a favorite of ski instructors who, as *Esquire* noted, "were exerting a tremendous influence on skiwear." Long before then, though, the cable-knit sweater was crafted for the fishermen of the rugged Aran Islands off the west coast of Ireland. The yarn is woven to create an effect of crisscrossing ropes. The cable pattern represented their fishing ropes and was believed to be a charm for good fortune at sea. Each fisherman's family had its own unique stitching, similar to a family crest, and it has been said that the fishermen knew, should they go overboard, that they could be identified by their sweaters alone. These days, though, the cable-knit works just as easily on dry land with a nice pair of jeans and suede bucks.

DAVID MAMET on
THE BLACK CASHMERE SWEATER

LIKE THE BLACK BERET (which one is always told is *blue*, but mine is black), the black cashmere turtleneck is a perfect garment (cf. Horst, Avedon, Irving Penn, et al.).

It accentuates the jawline, or in its absence, suggests it and, by extension, character.

It frames the face; it renders the torso more unitary and shapely; it warms; it can be worn casually or under the sport coat or suit as the closest approximation to the required-but-absent shirt and tie in that contest one will likely but not necessarily lose to the maître d'....I have tucked the sweater into my jeans, cinched the belt tight, turned the tweed cap brim-to-the-back, and felt the complete Martin Eden.

Such an *ensemble* will make one look good, or as good as one is ever going to look, and, therefore, make one feel good. No wonder I associate the sweater with love: It shares its job description....

We were plagued in philosophy class by the question of the Hammer: The handle breaks, and we replace the handle. Later, the head breaks, and we replace the head. Is it now the same hammer? The question of the Hammer could be argued yea or nay, but the moths have eaten my black sweater, and when the new one comes out of the box, it will be, by acclimation, by courtesy, and in fact, my same black cashmere turtleneck.

So doth philosophy serve Humankind. *Shantih.*

Originally published in full as "Diary of a Sweater," Esquire, May 1996.

{ *The* RULES }
•
IF YOU CAN'T PUT YOUR ARMS ALL THE WAY DOWN AT YOUR SIDES,
then your sweater's way too thick.

ALBERT EINSTEIN AND THE V-NECK SWEATER

➤ The world of academia may not be the first place to look for forward-thinking style, but many an intellectual has his own dress code based on comfort and simplicity. When Albert Einstein pulled a classic V-neck sweater over an open-collar shirt in the 1940s, little did he know he'd be making sartorial history with a utilitarian (let's call it rumpled) ensemble that still looks relatively modern. Costume designers soon calculated that putting a star in a V-neck sweater—Rock Hudson and James Dean included—conveyed instant smarts.

How to Wear a Sweater to the Office

While we've happily bid farewell (and R.I.P.) to the term *casual Fridays*, sometimes the prospect of donning yet another dress shirt and tie is almost enough to make you crave a pink slip. It's still possible to wear a sweater with a suit or sport jacket to work, particularly if you're employed in one of the so-called creative professions. Whether it's a V-neck, crewneck, or contemporary zip-front sweater, knitwear for the workplace should be of high quality—linen or fine-gauge cotton in summer, merino wool or cashmere in winter—and never misshapen or showing signs of wear. To keep the look dressed up instead of down, pair with classics like well-cut trousers, a great leather belt, and polished loafers.

THE V-NECK

You can't go wrong with a fine wool or cashmere V-neck worn with a plaid wool blazer and good wool trousers (see the Duke of Windsor, p. 195). Extra credit: A bright contrasting tie and striped shirt. Dress down with cords or jeans.

THE POLO

A white or light-color linen polo sweater paired with a khaki suit is a summer classic for occasions when a shirt and tie aren't obligatory. Alternatively, wear it with linen or khaki trousers, a plaid sport coat, and suede dress loafers.

THE ZIP-FRONT

Worn under a suit in winter, a fine-gauge zip-front sweater adds warmth with style. Leave the neck open to show off your shirt and tie. For a dose of Italian *sprezzatura*, look for beautiful detailing, like a color lining or contrast collar.

{ *The RULES* }
•
EVEN NED BEATTY LOOKS GOOD IN A BLACK TURTLENECK SWEATER.
Every man does. Buy one. Wear it.

The *Unnecessary* Sweater

You're going to a party. Outdoors. Maybe you'll need a sweater. Maybe not. If you're stuck holding it, these are the best of the bad options.

THE ARM TUCK

Why it's good: You won't stretch out the arms of your sweater by pulling them into knots. Why it's bad: Restricts your arm movement and ties up a hand that could be carrying a cocktail. What you're telling people: "God, I wish I hadn't brought this thing."

THE WAIST CINCH

Why it's good: Practical and inconspicuous. Why it's bad: It pads your waist with a few inches, and if knotted too tightly, it can damage the sweater. What you're telling people: "I am pragmatic and just might need this later. Where's the bar?"

THE THURSTON HOWELL III

Why it's good: Surprisingly comfortable (seriously), and if tied loosely, it won't fray your sweater. Why it's bad: People will think you look like an asshole, and there's a good chance they'll be right. What you're telling people: "I'd rather be in Nantucket."

THE BIKE MESSENGER

Why it's good: It puts a fresh, youthful spin on the Thurston Howell III. Why it's bad: Too hip by half. What you're telling people: "I bought this sweater on sale at Urban Outfitters, along with a sweet beanbag and some sandalwood incense."

HOW TO BUY CASHMERE

LOTS OF THINGS BILL THEMSELVES AS "PURE CASHMERE," but there's a reason some cashmere sweaters cost $90 and others cost ten times as much. The best variety comes from Mongolia and northern China and is called long staple cashmere, meaning the individual fibers measure at least 1.4 inches in length. (Rule number one: The longer the fiber, the better the fabric.) These strands can be twisted into especially strong, featherlight yarns, and the subsequent dyeing, weaving, and finishing processes are precisely monitored to ensure quality. Manufacturers pay upwards of $100 per kilogram for the good stuff—barely enough to make a single suit jacket.

Due to rising demand, it's now common to find bales of "pure cashmere" that contain a percentage of far cheaper lamb's wool; some of these lesser blends are coated with an emulsion that imparts the soft hand of top-quality cashmere but also gives the fabric a greasy residue. (Rule number two: Rub your fingers together after handling your prospective purchase to check for said residue.) Unfortunately, there's no universal manufacturer's symbol for high-quality cashmere, but most high-end brands have staked a reputation on carrying only the real thing. Sure, the prices are high, but that leads to our third and final rule: You get what you pay for.

THE ENDORSEMENT:

THE GRAY UNDERSHIRT

IN THE GRAND SCHEME OF THINGS, the color of one's undershirts may seem like a minor matter. Selecting your college, your spouse, your next tattoo—those are serious choices. Undershirts are simply what you use to soak up your sweat and protect your shirts from your body. That being said, the next time you're in the market for new ones, allow us to suggest a light-gray one (or, in the words of clothing catalogs, "heather" or "oatmeal"). Its biggest benefit is that, unlike a white undershirt, it doesn't show through light-colored dress shirts. This, our eighth-grade science education tells us, owes to the fact that gray reflects less light than white, so when a ray of light hits a fine oxford cloth, a gray undershirt will absorb it while a white undershirt will reflect it. The particular style of undershirt is negotiable. A crewneck provides complete protection from your body but requires you to button up and wear a tie (unless you like to leave your collar open to show the top of your undershirt, to which we say: Don't). A V-neck, meanwhile, allows you to go tieless but doesn't shield the shirt from chest perspiration, resulting in a smattering of sweat. In any case, we'd advise against the wifebeater. Gray or white, it does little to soak up underarm perspiration, and the ribs usually show through your outer shirt. Plus, they don't call it a wifebeater for nothing.

{ *The RULES* }

•

FITTED IS GOOD. Snug is dicey. Tight is just wrong.

•

THE MAN WHO IMPARTS OPINIONS VIA T-SHIRT has neither the intelligence to form a cogent opinion nor the good sense to keep it to himself.

•

EVERYTHING LOOKS BETTER WITH AGE. Except for white T-shirts. Those look best new.

•

TO OUR KNOWLEDGE, TANK DRIVERS never wore tank tops. If they did, we might like them better.

•

ALTHOUGH YOUR GIRL-FRIEND may appreciate that not washing your shirt makes it smell more like "you," your coworkers don't.

IF YOU'VE GOT A T-SHIRT WITH BLOODSTAINS ALL OVER IT, MAYBE LAUNDRY ISN'T YOUR BIGGEST PROBLEM.

—Jerry Seinfeld

JOHNNY DEPP AND THE WHITE T-SHIRT

➤ *Leave it to Depp, who fueled his career on the lure of outcasts and pirates (with an early pit stop in rock 'n' roll), to remind us just what drew American men to the plain white T-shirt. When another rebel, Marlon Brando, wore one in the 1951 movie* A Streetcar Named Desire, *he made fashion and retail history: The humble undergarment became an instant sportswear classic, and more than 180 million were sold by the end of the year.*

D AVERY

INSTANT FROZEN

ICE CREAM

WHERE TO FIND THE PERFECT FIT

SOMETIMES IT PAYS to be average. The great egalitarian principle of off-the-rack clothing—regular fit at a regular price—puts the average-sized guy with, say, a 15-inch neck and a 33-inch sleeve square in fashion's strike zone. But no matter what your lady tells her girlfriends, few of us measure out as Mr. Average.

And while you can fake your measurements a little with a tie, casual shirt, or pair of jeans, a dress shirt that's too tight can leave you blue in the face. So what do you do if you can't get the right fit off the rack? If nature has blessed you with a 17.5-inch neck and a pair of 32-inch arms, there are now options, as the custom shirts once reserved for the few are now available to the many.

The first time you wear a custom-made shirt, you will notice a few things. Your left cuff might run a bit larger than your right to compensate for your wristwatch. Your buttons will feel sturdier and stronger because they've been carefully stitched onto the fabric by a human hand. You will like it more than your other shirts because it is *your* shirt: From the color and pattern to the cuffs and the button style, you chose the details. You will feel more comfortable because, after the tailors have taken more than a dozen measurements and adjusted the shirt to your body over the course of two or three fittings, nothing will tug or sag with movement. You will look better because tailors can compensate for, and even hide, many physical shortcomings and because they've been trained to pair different kinds of collars with different face shapes. You will feel smarter because while a bespoke shirt may cost a little more money, you'll know that your hand-stitched shirt will probably last longer than anything made by a machine, and you'll end up saving money in the end. Finally, you may feel a little bit sorry, because after you wear a custom-made shirt for the first time, you'll wish every other shirt you own felt the same way.

A REMARKABLY DETAILED GUIDE TO

IRONING A SHIRT

FIG. A

FIG. B

FIG. C

FIG. D

1. START WITH THE BACK of the unbuttoned shirt flat on the board and the sleeves hanging down either side of the rounded end. Press using gentle circular motions. Use steam if needed (usually it's best if the shirt is not bone-dry—especially with cotton). Work away from the center to the side seams. *{ FIG. A }*

2. SELECT A SLEEVE, placing the underarm seam straight along the board and nearest to you. Smooth it out, holding it tight and flat while you firmly press the seam itself. Work away from the seam, being careful to sharpen any pleats. Repeat with the other sleeve. *{ FIG. B }*

3. MOVE ON TO THE CUFFS, opening them completely faceup (the side with the button on it). Iron from the sleeve edge of the cuff, working out toward the ends and sides of the cuff.

4. OPEN DOUBLE CUFFS completely and work in the same way. Press a sharp fold in the cuff only after you have pressed it open. Do not press the folded-back cuff flat. The only crease should be the one around the very end of the cuff.

5. MOVE ON TO THE FRONT of the shirt, laying each side flat and smoothing it out. Work around the buttons, taking care to press the plackets (the strips where buttons and buttonholes are placed) on both sides firmly. Work away from the plackets toward the side seams. *{ FIG. C }*

6. OPEN THE COLLAR faceup and lay it fully flat. Working from the outside edge of the collar, use tiny circular movements to avoid creasing the cotton against the stitching on the edge of the collar, which would be obvious and unsightly. Keep the iron pointed toward the shirt label. Fold the collar down and press in the top ridge firmly with your fingers. *{ FIG. D }*

How to Clean a Sweater

Washing a sweater is easily done at home, but it needs to be done by hand. Hand-washing knitwear is the best way to maintain its original luster and softness. Dry cleaning puts a shorter life span on knitwear, especially cashmere. Believe it or not, a gentle hair shampoo is ideal for most wool sweaters. Woolite is better for cashmere. Fill a well-scrubbed sink with lukewarm water and add about a capful of soap. Let the sweater soak for approximately fifteen minutes, then drain and rinse until the water runs clear. Gently press out excess water, by making a ball that looks like an uncooked loaf of bread, and then spread the sweater out flat on a towel, returning it as close to its original shape as possible, and allow it to dry.

An **ILLUSTRATED GUIDE** *to* **FOLDING**

THE T-SHIRT

{1}
Lay shirt faceup. Pinch shoulder with your left hand and chest with your right.

{2}
Crossing left hand over right, pinch the shoulder and the bottom hem together.

{3}
Lift the shirt, uncross your hands, and pull the shirt taut. Shake it and fold over.

{4}
Lay the shirt down faceup, and smooth and straighten accordingly.

THE SWEATER

{1}
Lay sweater facedown with arms spread. Smooth out any wrinkles.

{2}
Touch the left sleeve to the bottom of the right hem.

{3}
Touch the right sleeve to the bottom of the left hem, making a neat rectangle.

{4}
Fold the top half over the lower half and straighten accordingly.

A STACK OF SHIRTS

{1}
Stack shirts faceup on top of one another, with arms spread.

{2}
Fold the bottom half of the stack under the top half.

{3}
Place one set of sleeves across the chest and fold the other across it.

{4}
Place stack of shirts directly in suitcase. Remove upon arrival and hang in closet.

Sew a Button!

1. Make a single stitch in the shirt only, about ⅛ of an inch long. Leave a three-inch end of loose thread.

2. Do the same again, but this time perpendicular to the last stitch to make a cross.

3. Thread the needle up through one hole in the button and down through the diagonally opposite hole. Hold the button about ⅛ inch away from the shirt throughout. Next time use the other holes. Repeat four times.

4. Wrap the thread tightly around the shank that has been created between the button and the cloth to create a tight pillar.

5. Push the needle through this pillar a couple of times. Cut the thread close to the pillar.

HOW TO CLEAN SHIRTS

•

While we all want clean clothes, there are better methods than dry cleaning. Shoddy dry cleaning can ruin a dress shirt. The process can damage the fibers and can give whites a yellow tint. Having your shirts laundered not only gets them clean without chemicals but doubles their life span, too. When laundering, specify that your shirts be hand ironed and with no starch, which adds to the deterioration of your shirts and is never completely removed when washed. A lot of cleaners don't offer hand ironing, so shop around. If you prefer to launder your own shirts, machine wash them in lukewarm water with a nonbleach detergent and hang them to dry near, but not on, a radiator, window, or another source of heat. Steam or iron them when they're almost dry.

....

The *SARTORIAL CANON*

》》》 • 《《《

The Shirt and the Sweater

....

BORRELLI
➤ Neapolitan Luigi Borrelli learned the art of the hand-sewn shirt in his mother's atelier and established his eponymous shirt-making company in 1957. Today the shirts are hand-finished by seamstresses who mostly work from their homes around Naples. Tailored in exquisite fabrics, each Borrelli shirt's detailing is superb, as is its close-to-the-torso fit. www.luigiborrelli.com

CHARLES TYRWHITT
➤ British shirtmaker Charles Tyrwhitt was founded in 1987 as a mail-order enterprise producing high-quality classic English dress shirts at lower prices than its competitors. Tyrwhitt subsequently opened a flagship on London's Jermyn Street but remains primarily an online retailer. It offers a wide range of styles and fabrics at reasonable prices. www.ctshirts.co.uk

LORO PIANA
➤ After almost two centuries as one of Italy's leading family-owned textile manufacturers, Loro Piana began producing its own finished luxury products in the 1980s. Today the company creates a wide range of knitwear, but its simple V-neck cashmere sweater, in traditional as well as offbeat colors, is a classic. www.loropiana.com

THOMAS PINK
➤ English haberdasher Thomas Pink is named after an eighteenth-century tailor, but the company was established by three Irish brothers in 1984 to rival the fabled shirtmakers of Jermyn Street. Pink's ready-to-wear shirts come in so many styles and fabrics that they offer arguable competition to their bespoke equivalents. www.thomaspink.com

TURNBULL & ASSER
➤ Perhaps the most celebrated of all Jermyn Street haberdashers, Turnbull & Asser was founded in 1885 and has supplied riotously colorful and boldly striped shirts to a who's-who clientele, including the present Prince of Wales. Turnbull & Asser's face-flattering collars are slightly larger than most, and their patented three-button cuff is a natty alternative to turnback styles. www.turnbullandasser.com

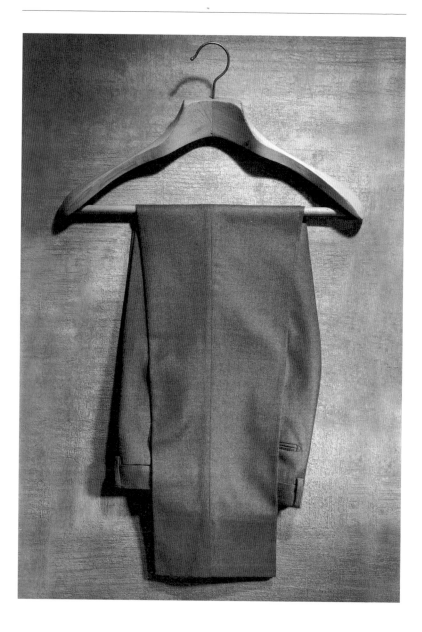

•

CHAPTER THREE

The Trousers

....

COULD ANYONE HAVE PREDICTED
*that denim "waist overalls," first made in 1873 by
Levi Strauss & Company to outfit prospectors
in the California gold rush, would become
the most influential—and profitable—garment ever
invented in America?* ➤

....

ESPECIALLY CONSIDERING THAT during the first half of the twentieth century, few men would have found jeans acceptable wear for anything other than manual labor—and we're not talking raking the sand trap or rolling the tennis court. It's hard to believe now, with boxer shorts sprouting from the backs of low-slung jeans on many a city street, but even in the dog days of summer, a relaxed outfit prior to the First World War might have consisted of a dark suit jacket worn with flannel or linen trousers.

EVEN WITH UNDERGARMENTS firmly under wraps, the postwar, youth-conscious society demanded a new ease and informality in dress. There were flappers to bed, speakeasies to frequent, violent workers' strikes, and raging unemployment—who needed fancy, restrictive suits? e.e. cummings even stopped using capital letters. Clearly, conventions of all sorts—sartorial included—were under siege. So came the need for more casual, stand-alone trousers that could be worn variously with blazers, sport jackets, shirts, and sweaters. Wool, both tropical weave in summer and flannel in winter, proved the most popular fabric for dressy sport trousers: in addition to retaining its shape well, wool is an efficient insulator in the cold, heat, and damp. Initially restricted to gray and white, it was soon available in a wide range of colors, though the most vivid hues were generally reserved for resort wear—except by the future Duke of Windsor, who often shocked the old guard with his brightly colored apparel.

EVEN IN CLASS-CONSCIOUS England, the privileged were snipping away at rigid dress codes, with trousers sending some powerful signals. Fashionable young men in the mid-1920s were switching overnight from slim, elegantly cut flannels to Oxford bags—enormously wide pleated trousers made popular by students at the eponymous university. British intellectuals were also adopting corduroy for town use in an effort to show solidarity with the farmhands who actually wore it to do real work. The humble, cut-pile cloth got the royal seal of approval when the Duke began to favor it, and corduroy has been a class-bending trouser ever since.

ALTHOUGH BLUE JEANS have never entirely lost their original sweat-of-the-brow utilitarianism, they gained cachet with city slickers as part of a fad for the romanticized Old West in the 1920s and 1930s. After the Second World War, the urban middle class began to adopt the sturdy, copper-riveted pants as leisure wear; movie idols like Marlon Brando and James Dean did the same, and the rest is history (see p. 97). As the Woodstock era faded, denim jeans began to lose their counterculture cool—but not their market share: Almost everybody everywhere, including Jimmy Carter and Ronald Reagan, had at least one pair of inexpensive dungarees, which became increasingly acceptable in all sorts of social and business situations. Andy Warhol even wore them with a tuxedo jacket to the White House in 1985, because, he said, "jeans are so easy."

THEN, IN THE LATE 1970s, jeans became "designer," as brands such as Gloria Vanderbilt, Fiorucci, and Calvin Klein began successfully chasing disco kids and denim dollars. Those designers did the early legwork for a new category of luxury pants, "premium" jeans, which suddenly appeared at the millennium's dawn. These high-end niche labels justify their elevated prices by producing limited-edition styles in high-quality fabric, often using artisanal production methods. Today the guy in the perfect 1950s five-pocket jeans is as likely to be a hipster with a trust fund as a rebel without a cause.

JAMES DEAN ALSO helped popularize America's other major contribution to men's below-the-belt sportswear, the casual cotton trousers known interchangeably as khakis or chinos. Both names reflect the pants' military origins (see p. 91). Like jeans, khakis are comfortable, inexpensive, and easy to care for, but they carry a more imposing set of associations than do working-class denim: The martial authority of the United States military and the faded grandeur of the British Raj. Perhaps that's why, paired with a sport coat, button-down shirt, and loafers, even threadbare khakis appear upright and proper; combined with a cashmere sweater, Sea-island cotton dress shirt, and elegant slip-ons, well-cut chinos look like a million bucks.

The TROUSER

What to look for in the perfect pair of pants

➤ THE FRENCH FLY

The nifty tab-and-button closure distinguishes a high-quality pair of trousers from your everyday variety. The zipper is attached to an extended waistband, which takes stress off the zipper and ensures that the front lies flat.

➤ LINED WAISTBAND

The waistband is lined to maintain its shape. Options include a split seam and a V-notch in the back so the trouser can be altered for a perfect fit.

➤ TAPED SEAMS

Seams are pressed, with their edges taped or piped for reinforcement and to keep them lying flat.

➤ LINING WHERE IT COUNTS

Good-quality trousers are lined through the crotch and often to just above the knees; the extra fabric ensures durability and plain old comfort.

➤ CUFFED VS. UNCUFFED

Cuffs add weight and draw attention to the line of the pants. If you're on the short side, forego the cuffs. Cuffed trousers should have a straight hem; an uncuffed hem should be longer in back, hitting the lower heel.

➤ PLEATS (OR NOT)

Pleats provide a touch of volume to the top of your trousers, which helps if you're a man of powerful build. Today, though, most trousers—even when they come with a suit—are flat fronted (see p. 88).

The Joy of Trousers

FLANNELS	CORDS	KHAKIS	JEANS

APPROPRIATE FOR			
Restaurants with $30 entrées	Attending football games, duck hunting	Country clubs, cocktail parties	Anything that doesn't involve a necktie
POSITIVELY ASSOCIATED WITH			
Cary Grant	Woody Allen	Steve McQueen	James Dean
NEGATIVELY ASSOCIATED WITH			
Old men	The French	Middle managers	Kids
STANDARD-BEARER			
Ralph Lauren	L. L. Bean	Dockers	Levi's
BEWARE OF			
Getting them wet	Superwide cords	Double pleats	Acid-wash
WHAT THEY SHOULD LOOK LIKE			
The same way you'd wear chinos, but with a crease	Pooling gently onto sneakers or aging brown wing tips	Without a pressed-in crease in sight	On the hips, neither tourniquet-tight nor circus-tent baggy

MICK JAGGER AND THE SKINNY PANT

➤ *Hipsters in Regency England sported skinny pants 150 years before the style went rock 'n' roll. In the 1950s, British "teddy boys" paved the way for the stovepipe trousers worn by the Mods and the Mick Jaggers of the following decade. Meanwhile, across the Channel, lean cinema stars like Marcello Mastroianni and Alain Delon popularized the new slim-cut Continental suits. But no matter what century, to look good in stovepipe trousers, you'd better be rail-thin, like perpetual rocker Jagger.*

The Three Dress Pants
YOU SHOULD OWN

Certain occasions—graduations, retirement dinners, bar mitzvahs—roll around as predictably as the sun rises in the west, but today's generation of man might just as predictably be stymied about what to wear. When a suit is not obligatory but you need to dress up, you should have trousers that can be teamed with a tailored jacket or sport coat. These days that often means good jeans or chinos, but here is a formidable triad of formal trouser options that pair up beautifully with that near-year-round wardrobe staple, the blue wool blazer. Yes, the combination is a classic, but that doesn't have to mean stodgy. To up your style quotient, add a bold orange tie or a beautiful cashmere sweater vest, and choose a shoe—like a brown wing tip—with personality.

GRAY TROPICAL WOOL	CHARCOAL GRAY FLANNEL	TAN CORDUROY
Tropical wool is the backbone of a dress-trouser corpus. Wear with a camel-color wool jacket and brown loafers or suede driving shoes for a look with Italian flair.	No wardrobe is complete without this staple. Period. In winter, add interest with a zip-front sweater, a striped shirt and tie, or a thick cable sweater and Chelsea boots.	Paired with a navy blazer, it's a no-brainer. To avoid looking like an Ivy League cliché, wear with a beautiful silk tie and monk-strap shoes, or substitute a bold tweed jacket.

HOW TO WEAR PANTS:
Or, the proper length at which to wear them

It is a constant debate, really. How far down on the shoe should the pant leg extend? There is, of course, a right and a wrong ankle altitude to which a man should extend the bottom of his trousers. Too long and your britches look borrowed. Too short and you'll get pegged a clam digger. And nobody digs for clams anymore. To help you out, here's our handy guide on how to wear your pants, the cuff edition. Take it with you to the tailor or photocopy this page and pin it to your closet door.

CUFFED SUIT PANTS	UNCUFFED SUIT PANTS	CHINOS	JEANS
The weight of the cuff (between 1.5 and 2 inches wide—anything more looks like you thought about it too much) straightens the trouser leg and gives it a clean line. The hem should not slope.	They should be long enough to give just a small break in the front crease. A perfect unbroken crease means that your pants are too short. The hem should slope toward the back.	Choose a leg length that will allow the bottom 3 inches to lie in an artfully crumpled heap on your casual shoes (see pp. 90–91).	Jeans should just cover the shoelaces and break on or around the ankle, but not to the same degree as chinos.

THE GOLDEN RULE

Nothing ruins the look of a smart suit so quickly as clumpy shoes.	Always wear formal shoes when you have trousers hemmed.	Essentially, they're casual trousers that should improve with age. That means your socks should never be seen. Let them hang.	We think denim always looks best with sneakers, boots, or rough wing tips. Too slim and elegant a shoe, with a thin sole and a pointy toe, just won't cut it.

The Pleat, Reconsidered:
A GUIDE TO PLEATED TROUSERS

SOMETIME IN THE PAST decade, pleated pants got a bad rap. Someone, somewhere—we suspect he was French—convinced the world that flat-front trousers were the ne plus ultra for modern men, whereas pleats were what Grandpa used to hide his beer belly. Pleats, however, have a lot going for them, particularly in the roominess department. They certainly come in handy when you're a man of a certain size and you're worried about one false move sundering your pants from crotch to waistband. Granted, they do nothing to tighten up your silhouette, but for most of us, our silhouettes weren't all that tight in the first place.

Although there are three basic types of pleated trousers, one rule holds for all: they must be worn on the waist, not the hips, or the pleats will pull open. For the same reason, they need to be fuller in the thigh, with legs that taper to a narrower ankle, which makes them generally inappropriate for contemporary slim-cut suits. That, of course, is not the case with flat-fronts.

FLAT-FRONT	REVERSE PLEATS	REGULAR PLEATS
More or less obligatory when it comes to modern slim-line suits. Optional details like slash or welted pockets vary the minimal look.	The pleats fold inward, producing near flat-front trousers. The most common pleated style of the past few years.	The pleats fold outward. Double pleats are probably more pleats than are warranted these days, but are still a relatively common style.

SPENCER TRACY AND THE PLEATED PANTS

➥ *Spencer Tracy, visiting with a black-costumed Laurence Olivier in 1951 on the set of* Father's Little Dividend, *sports a white jacket and the deeply pleated slacks that, in various guises, characterized four decades of menswear. The ballooning pants were descendents of Oxford bags, comically wide trousers that were popularized by students at the English university during the 1920s. The über-baggy style quickly disappeared, but Hollywood embraced the full cut, and its influence lives on in the form of pleated dress pants.*

THE ANATOMY OF

The Khaki Pant

No arguments, gentlemen: Khakis are one of America's greatest contributions to the world of style. Here, what makes them right:

1. THE COLOR
Khaki is a color. Chinos are a pair of pants. Know the difference but feel free to use the terms interchangeably.

2. RELAXED FIT
With noticeably wider legs and no sign of a crease, relaxed-fit pants look loose and athletic and may even have some fraying at the cuffs.

3. THE CRUMPLE FACTOR
Some light wrinkling and a slouchy construction typify the most casual breed of khakis. Wash them only when absolutely necessary. Creases are just another way of saying your khaki pants have been ironed. They also imply that you iron your socks (see Khaki Rule #2, opposite).

4. POCKETS
The best khakis have four pockets. Anything more or less and you're asking for trouble.

5. PLEATS AND CUFFS
Both add formality, as does a tab closure at the waist. Cuffs range from a light inch-and-a-quarter- to a two-inch-thick band, and they're best for men with long legs. If we were sticklers about it, we'd say no pleats and no cuffs. But the beauty of chinos is that it's up to you.

{ *The* CLASSICS }
The Dockers K-1 Chino

IS THE CHINO CASUAL OR FORMAL? For most Americans, it's both. But to stand as America's quintessential casual dress pants, the chino took a circuitous route. According to fashion legend, GIs returning from the Philippines in the years following the Spanish-American War in 1898 brought home light, tough pants made of a Chinese cotton twill. (*Chino* is Spanish for Chinese.) The U.S. military made much use of these economical yet functional pants. Made without pleats and with straight legs, the pants it created in 1932 proved as durable as they were comfortable, a boon during wartime shortages. The U.S. Navy approved khakis for off-duty wear in 1942, and the American public got to see sailors on leave in the versatile pants for the first time. Dockers' K-1 is a faithful re-creation of the military chino, complete with the original reinforced bar stitching, hook-and-eye closure, button fly, and hidden coin pocket.

The Most
UNDERRATED PANT

Despite its salt-of-the-earth connotations, America's official trouser has its nuances

. . . .

KHAKI RULE #1
Never roll the cuffs up to your calves like clamdiggers unless you are actually digging for clams.

. . . .

KHAKI RULE #2
Khaki is Hindi for "dust." Pure, natural, unenhanced earth. With that in mind, remember: A crease down the front of a pair of khakis adds fifteen years to the age of the wearer.

. . . .

KHAKI RULE #3
Think of your khakis as a leather briefcase. That first scar will break your heart, but you'll learn that they are at their lived-in best just before they disintegrate.

. . . .

KHAKI RULE #4
Unless you're on safari, limit the number of khaki items in your outfit to one. Better yet, apply this rule even while on safari.

. . . .

KHAKI RULE #5
Khakis are the most comfortable pants to sleep in. And sleeping in them makes them more comfortable.

. . . .

KHAKI RULE #6
Jack Kerouac wore khakis. So did Steve McQueen, who tried to jump over the Swiss border in khakis. He failed. But it wasn't his pants' fault.

GEORGE CLOONEY AND THE KHAKI PANT

➤ *George Clooney certainly is not the first movie star to wear khakis, but he pulls off the look so effortlessly—with a black T-shirt, leather lace-ups, and no socks—that it's as though he reinvented casual cool (movie-star good looks and an athletic build don't hurt). The military origins of khakis may lend a tactical quality to these classic pants, but on Clooney they're a world away from the starchy military style of Douglas MacArthur and his fellow generals.*

THE ANATOMY OF

Jeans

A celebration of history's most enduring pair of trousers

1. THE FIFTH POCKET
Jeans just don't look right without a fifth pocket—a safe, snug place to store beer money.

2. COPPER RIVETS
First patented in 1973 by Levi Strauss & Co. and a Latvian–born tailor from Nevada, rivets originally reinforced pockets and extended the life of the pant. Today they remain on most brands, part of the jean's DNA.

3. BUTTON FLY
Though the button fly can be a pain— especially with stiff jeans—it's the best way to pay homage to denim's hard- laboring heritage.

4. DIRT
Fashion has decreed that dirt will add to the mystery of your jeans. There are a lot of bad practitioners of the art of dirtying. Blobs and stains that are too uniform don't look right. And if the stain is too yellow, stay away. The right amount of fake dirt, though, will add to your intrigue.

5. LEG SHAPE
Flared or boot cut, straight or baggy, the lower leg defines what shoes you can wear. And what kind of man you are. But they shouldn't flare out like some twisted Travolta flashback—they should form to your contours like a good sweater.

QUESTIONS and ANSWERS FOR a MAN in DENIM

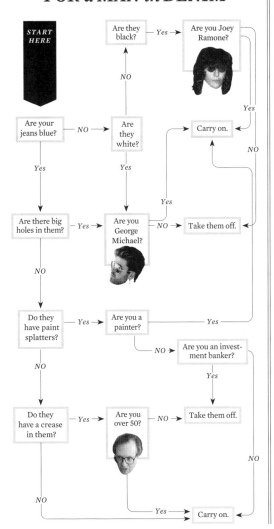

START HERE

Are your jeans blue? — NO → Are they white?

Are they white? — NO → Are they black?

Are they black? — Yes → Are you Joey Ramone?

Are you Joey Ramone? — Yes → Carry on.

Are you Joey Ramone? — NO → Take them off.

Are they white? — Yes → Are you George Michael?

Are your jeans blue? — Yes → Are there big holes in them?

Are there big holes in them? — Yes → Are you George Michael?

Are you George Michael? — Yes → Carry on.

Are you George Michael? — NO → Take them off.

Are there big holes in them? — NO → Do they have paint splatters?

Do they have paint splatters? — Yes → Are you a painter?

Are you a painter? — Yes → Carry on.

Are you a painter? — NO → Are you an investment banker?

Are you an investment banker? — Yes → Take them off.

Are you an investment banker? — NO → Carry on.

Do they have paint splatters? — NO → Do they have a crease in them?

Do they have a crease in them? — Yes → Are you over 50?

Are you over 50? — Yes → Carry on.

Are you over 50? — NO → Take them off.

Do they have a crease in them? — NO → Carry on.

HOW NOT TO WEAR JEANS

THE GRANDPA

THE LOW RIDER

THE WEEKENDER

THE BON JOVI

THE WEDGIE

RONALD REAGAN AND THE CLASSIC JEAN
➤ *A fresh-faced, dungaree-clad Ronald Reagan here reminds us why we love jeans—they are as quintessentially American as dusty farmland and gas-guzzling automobiles. Denim didn't always signal social rebellion or fashion-label cultishness. As any Levi's fan knows, jeans appeared 150 years ago as indestructible work trousers for prospectors in the California gold rush. Those humble roots are ones this publicity shot would have us believe the shovel-wielding movie star and future president shared.*

{ *The* CLASSICS }
Levi's

YOU COULD SAY it all started in the seventeenth century in the town of Nîmes, France, where a durable cloth was being woven called *serge de Nîmes* (denim, get it?). But the famous story of Levi's began in 1872, when a tailor by the name of Jacob Davis in Reno, Nevada, made a pair of work pants with copper rivets to strengthen the pocket corners. In 1873, Levi Strauss, a German-born cloth merchant from San Francisco, along with his customer Davis, pieced together sixty-eight dollars to patent the riveted work pants. The 501 label was added in 1890; the famous red pocket tab in 1936. And the double line of stitching on each back pocket is one of the oldest surviving trademarks in clothing. In the 1950s and 1960s, thanks to powerfully attractive, Levi's-sporting movie rebels like Marlon Brando and James Dean, jeans and a T-shirt or leather jacket became the uniform of the emerging youth culture. In 2003 the world's oldest pair of Levi's was purchased by Levi Strauss & Co. for its archive. Originally woven in a New Hampshire mill, the denim dates to the 1880s.

5 Tips for When You Buy
DENIM

1 } The heaviest acceptable weight for denim is around fourteen ounces per square yard (Levi's 501's weigh in at 13.75 ounces), although modern denim can go as light as seven ounces per square yard. Below seven ounces, it's chambray.

2 } The two measurements you need when buying denim are waist and inseam, in that order. Your inseam is measured from crotch to anklebone. Your waist is actually your hip measurement, since only murderers wear their jeans pulled up to their belly button.

3 } Always say no to stretch denim, black denim, and rhinestones.

4 } Never use a slim or too-posh belt with jeans. Wear one that looks like it could cope with heavy work.

5 } The current trend is distressed mid- and dark-blue denim with a softer, lived-in feel. However, the fashion-forward trend is toward stiffer, classic fourteen-ounce denim in dark finishes.

Sweatpants

Q *Is it ever okay to wear them? At what age should you stop? Does the same go for drawstring pants?*
If you're gearing up for a workout, sweatpants are the best thing to wear no matter how old you are. They're also ideal for shoveling the drive and running to the store—just don't wear 'em to work (unless you work at Gold's Gym), and avoid the kind with elastic at the bottom, which will gather tight around your sad little ankles and make you look chicken-legged.

Nonathletic drawstring pants are technically acceptable for male types—the same way that leather sandals are. Meaning: consider very, very carefully. Wear them and you may border on the International Male–catalog look. We'd argue that there's only one time a guy can pull off a pair of drawstring pants: bedtime.

{ *The RULES* }
•
BEFORE YOU WASH YOUR JEAN SHORTS, *pretreat them by throwing them away.*

A FEW WORDS ON SHORTS

Forget opening day at the ballpark or last-minute meetings with your accountant—the surest sign that spring has arrived is kneecaps as far as the eye can see, with people breaking out their shorts and settling in for a few months of barelegged recklessness.

This is how shorts are supposed to fit: not too long, not too short, and hitting just above the knee. Don't be one of those guys who wears really short shorts and doesn't care that his boxers are peeking out of the bottom. And don't wear really long ones, either, since those are not, in fact, shorts but short pants. There's a big difference. Huge.

And there's the question of patterns. We're not categorically against these madras shorts, especially on the golf course, but simple khaki shorts can't be beat. And unless you're attending a wedding in Bermuda, don't even think about wearing madras shorts with a madras blazer—even better, don't do it at all, ever (see p. 198).

The Savile Row Fold

Need to stop your suit trousers from falling off their hangers? Try the Savile Row fold, perfected over generations by the staff at London's finest custom-tailoring emporiums. Start with the trousers upside down and straddling the hanger you choose. Fold one leg in through the hanger, dropping the bottom hem in between until it sits just above the crotch. Fold the second trouser leg over the first and through the hanger. Shake the hanger. Nothing happens. Clever, isn't it?

...AND OTHER IDEAS FOR HANGING PANTS

The ideal hangers for pants are the sort with two spring-loaded slats of wood that grip the hem of the trousers so that they hang upside down. This allows creases and side hems to strengthen under gravitational pull.

{ The RULES }

•

GRAY FLANNEL PANTS ARE THE NAVY BLAZER OF COLD-WEATHER TROUSERS. *They go just as well with a T-shirt as with a white oxford and tie, so you might want to think about stocking up.*

•

LET THE SOCKS MATCH THE PANTS, NOT THE SHOES.

What Not to Put in Your
PANTS POCKETS

EYEWEAR
Looks bad. Feels bad.
Just plain bad.

PDA, CELL PHONE
Your pockets are not your
mobile office.

INK PEN
Especially not on a plane.

BULGING KEY CHAIN
And lose the mini
bottle-opener.

....

The *SARTORIAL CANON*

≫ • ≪

The Trousers

....

DOCKERS	➤ Introduced by Levi Strauss in the mid-1980s, Dockers seemed ill-fated to become a code word for suburban frumpiness. Worn the right way, however—pleatless, cuffless, slim fitting, ankle skimming—with a pair of loafers, Dockers are great looking, inexpensive casual trousers. And their K-1 khaki is an unassailable classic (see p. 91). If you're that concerned, remove the label on the rear end. www.us.dockers.com
ETRO	➤ Etro, a family-run Milanese textile and fashion company started in 1968, makes menswear for the urban dandy. Designed by Kean Etro, son of founder Gimmo, the beautifully tailored clothing splashes color and pattern over shirts, jackets, and superb slim-cut trousers. www.etro.com
LEVI'S	➤ Genderless, classless, and ageless, Levi's last forever, and they look good on almost everybody. No American wardrobe is complete without a pair. What's more, in an age when premium jeans sell for hundreds of dollars, the price of a pair of Levi's 501 jeans has actually fallen twenty dollars over the past decade. Of course, economy is only one of many reasons to love the archetypal five-pocket dungarees. www.levisstore.com
MICHAEL BASTIAN	➤ Bastian, a former men's fashion director at Bergdorf Goodman, launched his own line of sportswear in 2006. Made in Italy, Bastian's preppy-sophisticate clothing melds European stylishness with American straightforwardness and comfort. His trousers are particularly successful—chinos, moleskins, twills, corduroys, and flannels in high-quality fabrics and expertly proportioned cuts. www.michaelbastiannyc.com
PAUL SMITH	➤ British designer Paul Smith has made a successful career of merging Carnaby Street with Savile Row. In that nonchalant English way, he takes traditional patterns and textures—pinstripes, plaids, houndstooths, tattersall checks, corduroy—and gives them a pleasingly eccentric twist. www.paulsmith.co.uk

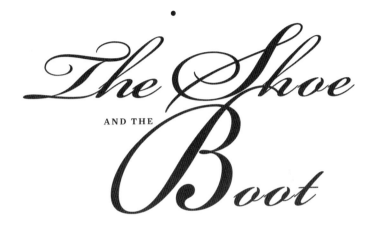

CHAPTER FOUR

The Shoe AND THE *Boot*

....

WHEN YOU OPEN YOUR CLOSET
in the morning, you should be presented with at least three good options for that day's footwear—assuming you haven't lost one of them under the sofa. You should have a dressy lace-up shoe, a half boot, and a casual, no-lace shoe, such as a loafer—or some combination of those three in the colors and styles you favor. ➠

....

ABOUT SNEAKERS: Your job may allow you to wear them to work, but condoning the practice is another thing. We're going to bet that if you are over thirty-five, you might occasionally experience a twinge of doubt when pulling on those Nikes or Pumas before you head out to the office. Heed your instincts. Wearing kicks to work is fine, if done with style (make sure the laces are spankin' white), and if you're not alone among your coworkers and your boss. But if you're serious about looking good, and being taken seriously, you've got to pick your moments—and sport those cap-toes when it counts.

NEVER MIND SPORTS—it was the exertions of military men, rather than athletes, that historically influenced men's footwear. In the early nineteenth century, the well-dressed man wore high boots in both town and country. Two popular styles, the Wellington and the Blucher, were named respectively after the British and Prussian field marshals—joint victors at Waterloo—who devised them. Wellington had his London shoemaker design a soft, close-fitting calfskin boot that was tough enough for battle yet sufficiently elegant for evening wear; it remained fashionable until the 1870s, but was immortalized as the "Wellie," a rubber farm boot introduced in France more than 150 years ago. The blucher was an ankle boot that laced in front over a tongue. The field marshal specified it for his troops because it was easy to get on and off; with the invention of metal eyelets in the 1820s, lacing and unlacing it became an even simpler and quicker matter.

DURING THE EARLY twentieth century, the oxford, whose many variants include the cap-toe, the wing-tip, the brogue, and the balmoral, was the quintessential and most successful gentleman's shoe, and it persists today as the working man's classic. The British dominated the world market for men's fine footwear between the two world wars, which meant a stylish shoe was an English-style shoe. Britain's cold, wet weather led to sturdy construction methods in which heavy leather uppers are stitched to thick welted soles, creating substantial, solid-looking shoes that perfectly complemented the period's broad-shouldered, wide-trousered suits. Those high-quality materials and workmanship were necessarily expensive, and they remain so. There's no way around the fact: Cheap shoes always and only look like cheap shoes, which is why the rich are referred to as well heeled.

IN TANDEM WITH the post-1980s trend toward slimmer suits, men's dress shoes have also been getting leaner, with narrower toes and thinner soles. Thus today's English or American oxford is a somewhat slighter shoe than its 1920s antecedent, though it's still likely to be stouter than its Italian counterpart. The Italians, coping with Mediterranean sun and a lifestyle that wasn't exactly stiff-upper-lip, began perfecting light, unconstructed, tailored clothing during the twentieth century and demanded similarly weightless and elegant footwear to go with it. When the country developed a ready-to-wear men's shoe industry after the Second World War, it largely dispensed with stitched-welt construction in favor of gluing fine calfskin uppers directly to single-thickness leather outsoles. Marked by superb hand-craftsmanship, slipper-like Italian shoes and thin-soled dress boots are especially appropriate companions for the newer suits with their trim trousers and pared-down silhouettes.

THE ITALIANS REFINED casual footwear, too, including an all-American classic, the penny loafer. The comfortable slip-on originated as a moccasin-style shoe handmade by Norwegian fishermen during their off-season. American tourists discovered it in the mid-1930s, and G. H. Bass first manufactured the Weejun in 1936 (drop the "Nor" from "Norwegian" and you get the derivation). Like blue jeans and the trench coat, the loafer became a timeless, genderless wardrobe staple—and a preppy cliché. Italian manufacturers, most famously Gucci, took the simple slip-on, upgraded the leather, thinned down the sole, elongated the toe, and replaced the coin slot with a gleaming bridle-bit seen on playboys and jet-setters since the 1970s. Today, with airline travel requiring all but stripping to your birthday suit, loafers are about the most practical all-around shoe you can buy. Just be sure to part with enough cash to acquire a great pair. After all, one of the first laws of fashion is that nothing undermines the effect of a perfectly good suit more unequivocally than a pair of shoddy lace-ups—or slip-ons.

The **DRESS SHOE***

A fine shoe, like a fine watch, combines mechanical precision with human artistry. And, as with a watch, a good pair of oxfords is a lifetime companion.

➤ APRON

A large overlay that covers the area where the toe meets the upper part of the foot.

➤ COUNTER

The half-moon-shaped piece of leather reinforcing the heel

➤ HEEL

The rear, padded area on the bottom of the foot, as well as the piece at the rear of the shoe that supports the heel cup. The heel should not slip off the wearer's foot.

➤ QUARTER

The continuous side and rear panel that forms the side of the shoe, extending from the vamp in front to the heel in the back.

➤ TOE BOX

The front portion of the shoe that covers the toes. It should have support protecting the toes and should be approximately a half inch longer than the length of the longest toe.

➤ TONGUE

A strip of leather running just under the laces of the shoe all the way to the opening, or throat.

➤ VAMP

The front part of the shoe that includes the toe box and the apron.

*And Other Shoe Terms You Should Know

➤ BROGUED

Refers to the holes in a wing-tip. They once went all the way through to let Scottish bog water out. The term is a nod to the shoe's origins in the Scottish Highlands (*bróg* is Gaelic for footwear).

➤ GOODYEAR WELT

The sole and the upper of the shoe are stitched together (not glued), resulting in the strongest bond in shoemaking. Because of its construction, a Goodyear welt lends itself to resoling many times over.

➤ LINER

The inside covering of the shoe. It should always be leather, since that's what will be touching your foot.

➤ PATINA

The subtle and desirable variation in color normally found in a pair of much-loved and much-polished old shoes.

➤ WING TIP

The distinctive avian, or peaked, shape of the toepiece of a pair of full brogues.

The Five Shoes Every Man Needs

The bottom of your closet should look something like this:

BLACK OXFORDS
The sensible bedrock of the grown man's shoe collection. These will get you through just about every family crisis and black-tie event life can throw at you—provided you keep them polished.

BROWN WING-TIPS
If black shoes mean business, then brown wing-tips mean...business. But less so. Look for a robust construction, but nothing so casual that you can't wear them with a suit. Ideally, you will eventually have two pairs of brown to your one pair of black.

LOAFERS
If you're an American, you need a loafer. Year-round, the official dress shoe of the United States is formal enough for the office and as casual as dress-down Friday should ever get.

CLASSIC BUCKS
Bucks have enjoyed continual renaissances, mainly because they make ideal partners for dark jeans and khakis. Consider them a semi-dress-up alternative to sneakers.

CLASSIC SNEAKERS
The sneaker holds a high place in the annals of American footwear. You need a pair in your closet. And we don't mean tennis sneakers. Or running sneakers. Or "hybrid" sneakers. We mean sneakers.

JACK LEMMON AND THE LOAFER

➤ *The loafer has been a classic since the debut of the moccasin-style Bass Weejun in 1936. A couple of decades later, refined by the Italians in featherweight leather or suede, dress loafers signaled Continental sophistication on everyone from Aristotle Onassis to Congolese premier Patrice Lumumba. In the 1950s, actor Jack Lemmon personified America's leisurely suburban style in a sport shirt, slacks, and a pair of polished black loafers, while Elvis frequently opted for a two-tone slip-on instead of blue suede shoes.*

DECODING THE DRESS SHOE

Footwear that toes the formal line

BLACK CAP-TOE OXFORD	BROWN WING-TIP BROGUE	BROWN MONK-STRAP	BROWN PLAIN-TOE DRESS LOAFER

THE HALLMARKS

A discreet toecap.	Peaked toecap and curving side seams with perforations.	A buckle-and-strap closure that replaces traditional eyelets and laces.	A slip-on with a high vamp and substanial sole.

VARIATIONS

Black calfskin is classic, but dark brown leather is pretty classy, too.	A refined European version—black or cordovan calf with a thin sole and a narrow, elongated toe.	Natty suede and the quirkier two-strap model.	Exotic leather or skin, the mark of a true dandy.

WEAR IT WITH

A good suit in fine worsted or flannel.	Any type of suit except black. With heavier fabrics like tweed and corduroy.	A serious worsted suit—and almost any other style of suit or tailored trouser.	A casual suit, or tailored trousers with a blazer or sport jacket.

WEAR IT TO

The boardroom. Weddings. Inaugurations. Funerals, including your own.	The office. A swank lunch. The polo field.	Work and play—it's a true chameleon.	The airport—you'll get through security faster and still look great when you arrive at your meeting.

WEAR IT AT YOUR OWN RISK

Anywhere except in town.	With a black suit.	On very formal occasions.	With pennies or horse bits.

THREE WAYS TO TIE YOUR SHOES

•

Mathematically speaking, there are millions of different ways to lace a shoe with six pairs of eyelets. But you could get by with three.

STRAIGHTLACED	CRISSCROSS	OVER-UNDER
Why: The neatest, most classic look. ***How:*** Run the lace through the lowest set of eyelets so that the ends come out the bottom of the upper. Run one end of the lace up the left side (so that it's hidden from view) and pull it through the top left eyelet; then pull the other end through the remaining eyelets so that the lace forms straight lines across the shoe.	***Why:*** Strong, lasting support. ***How:*** Run the lace through the lowest set of eyelets so that the ends come out the bottom of the upper. Cross the ends over each other and enter the next set of eyelets from the bottom. Pull through the ends and enter the next set of eyelets from the top. Repeat these steps with the remaining eyelets.	***Why:*** Comfortable and easy on the foot. ***How:*** Run the lace through the lowest set of eyelets so that the ends come out the top of the upper. Then cross the ends and enter the next set of eyelets from the bottom. Pull through and continue to cross the ends of the lace while entering each eyelet from the bottom.

straightlaced \straˉt·laˉst\ *adj* : **1.** A common colloquialism originating in England in 1554 used to describe an individual who exhibits excessively reserved or, some would say, uptight behavior. Syn: *prude, stick-in-the-mud, wet blanket.* **2.** A method of fastening shoes and other garments with laces that bind two separate pieces by spanning them straight across rather than in a crisscross pattern. A common technique used by Europeans to lace their shoes, it results in a tighter, stronger binding. Used by well-bosomed Victorian women to cinch their corsets. Also employed by British soldiers looking for a more secure way to fasten their boots.

THE STYLE DEFINITION: STRAIGHTLACED

FRED ASTAIRE AND TWO-TONE SHOES
➤ *Two-tone shoes are not for the retiring—they don't call them "spectators" for nothing. They've long been popular with dandies and hoofers, or both: Fred Astaire sported a version in 1942's You Were Never Lovelier with Rita Hayworth. Worn with white flannel trousers, two-tones became fashionable at posh resorts before the First World War. In the 1920s, American golfers, following the Duke of Windsor's lead, brought them to the greens. More recently, a pair anchored Johnny Depp's 1930s French Riviera–inspired ensemble at a movie premiere.*

The Mysteries of Suede Shoes

Q *How should I wear them?*

In 1924 the Prince of Wales, that dapper risk taker, scandalized Long Island's Meadowbrook Country Club by sporting brown suede shoes with his flannel suit. Some called them brothel creepers. By the 1930s, however, suede shoes were the mark of a real gentleman. Today they signify a sophisticated and individualistic dresser, someone who cares about his feet as much as the rest of his body.

Q *How do I know if they're well made?*

As with any investment, you should quiz the salesman. If he can't answer as to the quality of the shoe, move on. The best suede is made from the reverse, or flesh, side of calfskin. Kidskin is also used for dressy shoes because of its fine nap. Don't confuse it with nubuck, which looks quite similar but is made from the exterior side of leather that has been buffed but is of lesser quality. Remember that a suede shoe is tactile footwear, so work the shoe through your hands. Examine it. You'll know it's a well-made pair if the soles and inner linings are leather and the components are stitched together rather than cemented. Cement-bound shoes will inevitably fall apart, leaving you feeling angry and looking tragic.

Q *Which style should I wear?*

First you must decide on color. The very nature of the suede shoe is understated, so no Siegfried-and-Roy pastels here, please. Go with chocolate, cognac, or black in the winter and something light brown or tan in the summer. As far as the style of the shoe goes, the most versatile are cap-toe lace-ups, monk-straps, and chukka boots because they all work admirably with both navy and gray suits. You can also throw them on with a pair of jeans, khakis, or corduroys just as easily. Call them the utility infielders of foot dressing.

HOW SHOULD I TAKE CARE OF THEM?

SUEDE IS TOUGHER THAN it looks. To keep your shoes in prime condition, occasionally apply a protective product. In addition, a pair of unvarnished shoe trees should be put in them when they're not on your feet. These will absorb perspiration and help them keep their shape. After wearing, simply brush with a soft-bristle brush (not a wire one, as it will wear away the nap); this should be a regular wearing procedure, kind of like changing your car's oil. In case they get lightly stained—and they most certainly will—you can brush them with a soft gum eraser, and that should do the trick. Then there's the dreaded drenched shoe. You're bound to run out of luck and have to watch your suede-covered feet suffer through a downpour. Don't fret. Stuff them with paper towels and put them in a dry place for twenty-four hours, then lightly brush back the nap and they'll be nursed back to health. Another handy homespun remedy: You can restore suede shoes by lightly steaming them over boiling water. Or you can leave it to a pro to steam-clean them for you.

> WITH A SUIT, ALWAYS WEAR BIG BRITISH SHOES, THE ONES WITH LARGE WELTS. THERE'S NOTHING WORSE THAN DAINTY LITTLE ITALIAN JOBS AT THE END OF THE LEG LINE.
>
> —*David Bowie*

A GUIDE TO BOOTS

GIVEN THAT THERE ARE BOOTS for all seasons, occasions, and purposes, it's surprising that most men don't wear them much, trudging through the snow or up a mountain excepted. But because many types of boots have slightly maverick origins, they can be a great way to give your style quotient a raffish kick.

The Dress Boot
Whether lace-up or slip-on, with discreet straps or without, a boot that can be worn with all but the most formal suit must be unembellished.

The Chelsea Boot
The ankle-high slip-on with a pointed toe and a zippered or elasticized side opening was a Mod staple in 1960s London. Worn with a slim suit, these boots will still give you a subtle British-invasion vibe. Casual versions may have rounder toes and more overall heft, and look good with jeans and cords.

The Desert Boot
Inspired by crepe-soled footwear worn by British servicemen in Egypt during World War II, the suede or soft-leather lace-up was adopted by American rappers in the 1990s as an alternative to the sneaker. Many contemporary takes on the classic desert boot are natty enough to take you from a creative day job to a nightclub.

The Chukka Boot
This more substantial, leather-soled relative of the desert book started life on the polo field. Its plain good looks are a fine complement to smart tailored sportswear and even casual suits.

THE BEATLES AND THE CHELSEA BOOT

➤ *As if the Beatles need another notch in their belt, the Fab Four are credited for popularizing the Chelsea boot—an ankle-high slip-on with elasticized gussets—although they wore a highly customized version that's more accurately called the Beatle boot. The Liverpudlians had London shoemakers Anello & Davide graft elements of the Spanish flamenco boot onto the traditional Chelsea model. Pair the boots with a Pierre Cardin–inspired collarless suit and you're ready for a British invasion.*

WILT CHAMBERLAIN AND THE HIGH-TOP SNEAKER
➤ *Until Kobe Bryant plays a regulation game in a pair of low-tech canvas-and-rubber Chucks, he's gotta give props to Wilt Chamberlain, also known for his scoring on and off the court. Wilt, a.k.a. the Big Dipper, first laced his high-tops for the Kansas Jayhawks in 1955, the beginning of a career that reinvented basketball. In the 1970s, punk rockers like the Ramones became fans of the sneakers, claiming them as part of their own impudently uncouth style.*

{ *The* CLASSICS }
The Chuck Taylor All Star

IN 1923, IN THE FIRST ITERATION of the modern shoe-endorsement deal, basketball evangelist Charles ("Chuck") Taylor signed on to promote Converse, partnering with the shoe company to make the Chuck Taylor All Star. A star high-school player in Indiana, Taylor knew his game: he had also been a journeyman jump shooter for eleven professional seasons. Converse added Taylor's signature to the ankle in 1932, and the canvas-and-rubber shoe has essentially remained the same since (though now it's available in nearly every color and zany pattern known to man). The All Star was the official shoe of the Olympics from 1936 to 1968, and Chucks have functioned off the court as the shoe of American youth for most of the past eighty years. Its devotees include quintessential American iconoclasts and mischief-makers from Dennis the Menace to Ferris Bueller, Iggy Pop, and Rocky Balboa.

Five things you didn't know about
SNEAKERS

{ 1 }
The NBA banned the first pair of Air Jordans from competition in 1985 because their black-and-red combination did not conform to obscure league uniform rules.

{ 2 }
In 2007, Americans purchased about $2.4 billion worth of athletic sneakers.

{ 3 }
Ethiopian Abebe Bikila won the 1960 Olympic marathon in Rome while running barefoot.

{ 4 }
In 1916, U.S. Rubber Company trademarked a new rubber-soled shoe. The name Peds was already taken, so it chose Keds instead. The first sneaker was born.

{ 5 }
For running shoes, the American Academy of Podiatric Sports Medicine recommends a size large enough so that you can fit one index finger between the end of your longest toe and the inside edge of the shoe.

BOB DENVER AND THE SANDAL

➤ *Sandals have been around almost since man walked upright, and they were a favorite with Jesus, the ultimate counterculture guy of his time. Somewhere along the line, they became relegated to beachwear and hippie style. In the 1968 film* The Sweet Ride, *Bob Denver, playing a jazz pianist mixed up with beach bums in Malibu, showed you don't have to be Gilligan to make a sandal a wardrobe staple. The sturdy retro styling of this pair leaves today's flip-flops in the dust.*

How a Shoe Should Fit

Squeezing into a suit that doesn't fit? We've all done it. Squeezing into a shoe that's too tight? Murder. Here's what you need to know to keep your feet happy.

AT THE HEEL: This is the one place where your shoe may hurt initially, but fear not. It'll subside. Your heel should rest comfortably against the back liner without slipping.

AT THE INSTEP: The tongue should rest lightly on the top of your foot, without the feeling of too much pressure.

AT THE TOE: Your longest toe should rest about a half inch from the front edge of the toe box. You should be able to wiggle your toes slightly.

AT THE ARCH: Extra support is fine here, but the shoe should not rise up so much that pressure is put on your arch.

{ *The RULES* }
•
NO ONE YOU WORK WITH SHOULD EVER see your toes or nipples. Please dress accordingly.

Shoe Size

Inches		Size
9 1/2	—	6.5
9 5/8	—	7
9 13/16	—	7.5
10	—	8
10 1/8	—	8.5
10 5/16	—	9
10 1/2	—	9.5
10 5/8	—	10
10 13/16	—	10.5
11	—	11
11 1/8	—	11.5
11 5/16	—	12
11 1/2	—	12.5
11 5/8	—	13
11 13/16	—	13.5
12	—	14

- Sit with your foot (in a sock) on a piece of paper with your shinbone at a slightly forward angle.
- Trace around your foot with a pencil.
- Draw parallel lines to mark the outermost points (width and length) of your foot.
- Measure the length to 1/16 of an inch.
- Do the same with your other foot.
- Choose the larger foot and subtract 1/16 to 1/8 of an inch from the measurement to allow for error.

POLISHING
The Materials
•

You'll need the right tools—just a few, but each with a crucial purpose.

SHOE POLISH
Kiwi wax-based polish is as good a brand as any other. (Cream polishes, applied with a brush, may be easier to use, but they won't give you the same shine.) You don't need every color under the sun. Black, of course; a chestnut or darker brown; and something middling or neutral for light-colored shoes.

WELT BRUSH
Looks like a toothbrush (and you can use one in its place). It's designed to get the grit out of the welt, the seam where the shoe's upper joins the sole. You'd be amazed how much dirt gets in there.

POLISHING CLOTH
In lint-free cotton or linen. Use the same one for putting on the polish that you use for buffing, regardless of the color you're using. And hang on to it: The longer you use the same cloth, the more it becomes suffused with rich oils and dyes.

POLISHING BRUSH
To get the high shine out of the shoe once you've got all that wax into the leather. Horsehair is recommended.

SOLE DRESSING
The edge of the sole takes a scuffing from doorjambs and sidewalks. Restore the pristine look of your shoes with edge dressing, applied with a small craft brush or a cotton swab.

HOW TO
POLISH A SHOE

{ 1 }
Wipe your shoes down with a damp cloth to remove superficial dirt and stains.

{ 2 }
Wet the welt brush and scrub out the entire welt strip.

{ 3 }
If the shoes need it, apply sole-edge dressing—carefully. If you get it on the uppers, it will stain them permanently. Let the edge dressing dry before going any further.

{ 4 }
Apply polish, using a circular rubbing motion. You don't need to slather it on. You don't need to be gentle. And the more you rub, the better. Let the polish dry. It should take about five minutes.

{ 5 }
Buff the entire shoe with a polishing brush. For extra gleam, hold the shoe between your knees and buff the toe vigorously with a lint-free cloth.

EMERGENCY MEASURES and LONG-TERM CARE

Shoes as Investments

CHEAP SHOES ARE A FALSE BARGAIN. They're made of glue, rubber, and low-grade leather, which often bears scars from shrubs, trees, and barbed wire (the normal hazards of bovine life), and which is rejected out of hand by reputable shoemakers. Good shoes begin with great leather, period. Be prepared to pay for it, down to the sole. Of course, once you have invested your hard-earned cash in a quality pair, you're going to want to hang on to them. Put a little time and effort into looking after them and they'll last longer—and be more comfortable—than any three pairs of cheap clodhoppers.

SHOE TREES

Using a wooden shoe tree is the easiest way to increase the life expectancy of a good pair of shoes. The devices maintain the shoes' shape because they mimic the last—a facsimile of your foot on which shoes are built. But more important, the wood absorbs leather-damaging moisture, which can discolor and crack a shoe as it dries—but only if you choose the less decorative unvarnished ones. Varnished trees look posh, but they don't properly draw moisture—i.e., sweat—out of the leather. Top marks go to unfinished cedar models with a split toe and a fully shaped heel: these ensure the closest possible fit between shoe and tree. Also, there's no need to own a pair of trees for each pair of shoes. The vital time for using them is the hour or two after you have removed the shoes from your feet. After that, the shoes will have returned to their natural architecture and the trees can be removed.

REPAIR WORK

Invest as much care in choosing a cobbler to resole or reheel your shoes as you did in purchasing them. To prevent permanent damage (or, at the least, outrageous repair costs), have all work done before it's absolutely necessary.

SUEDE

Suede shoes are in a category of their own, since you cannot polish away scuff marks. See p. 113 for detailed tips.

WET SHOES

Stuff soaking-wet shoes with newspaper and dry them away from direct heat. Direct heat can dry the leather too fast, causing it to crack—and once that happens, nothing can save your shoes.

SALT STAINS

The traditional remedy for road-salt stains is a little vinegar and water, applied sparingly.

{ *The RULES* }

ALWAYS BUY YOUR SHOES AFTER 2:00 p.m., when your feet have swollen to their maximum measurement.

A MAN NEEDS BUT ONE SET OF SHOE TREES. Leave them in the last pair you wore, then remove when necessary.

....

The SARTORIAL CANON

⫸ • ⫷

The Shoe and the Boot

....

ALLEN EDMONDS ➤ Wisconsin-based shoemaker Allen Edmonds was founded in 1922 and remains one of the few high-quality American shoemakers that still manufactures in the United States. Using Goodyear welt construction, the company produces elegant dress shoes at a reasonable cost. It recently introduced a new line of calfskin shoes handcrafted entirely in Italy, with a sleek, European feel. www.allenedmonds.com

BERLUTI ➤ Italian bespoke shoemaker Alessandro Berluti opened his fabled Paris atelier in 1895; Toulouse-Lautrec, John F. Kennedy, and Andy Warhol have all been clients since then. Berluti offers deeply burnished ready-to-wear shoes in addition to the company's superbly elegant custom shoes, which take several weeks to make. www.berluti.com

CHURCH'S ➤ Church's is the quintessential traditional British shoemaker, established in Northampton in 1873. All of its footwear is made by hand using Goodyear welting, and the company offers famously comprehensive repair and made-to-order services. Prada acquired Church's in 1999 but appears intent on maintaining the company's distinctive profile. www.church-footwear.com

JOHN LOBB ➤ The world's most famous bespoke shoemaker, John Lobb was founded in London in 1849 and opened a Paris branch in 1901. In 1976, Hermès acquired all but the original London shop—which is still a made-to-order-only business run by the great grandson of the founder—and introduced a Lobb ready-to-wear line. www.johnlobbltd.co.uk; www.johnlobb.com

J. M. WESTON ➤ Established in 1891 in Limoges, France, J. M. Weston produces handmade footwear using Goodyear welt construction. Weston offers elegant dress shoes and a wide selection of lighter, contemporary casual shoes, some of which are reinterpretations of vintage styles from the company's archives. www.jmweston.com

•

CHAPTER FIVE

The Coat

AND OTHER

Outerwear

MEN HAVE ALWAYS NEEDED A TRUSTY
*outer garment to wear over our regular kits for extra
protection from cold or wet weather. More than with any
other garment, outerwear is a matter of basic survival
whose use dates back to Gronk and Shadd, and even to
cavemen who never had a TV show.* ➤

TODAY CASUAL COMFORT and versatility most often trump formality, thanks mainly to technical improvements in textiles. Puffy-yet-sleek ski parkas, which take advantage of microfiber shells and synthetic-down insulation, have descended from the slopes to become an urban fashion staple, as have less insulated snowboarding shells. Yet when you're wearing a well-made suit with English or Italian shoes with an heirloom price tag, donning one of these pieces of technical gear can be akin to slapping mag wheels on your vintage TR-6. Judge your needs carefully: Usually there's a more appropriate choice for the office, unless there's a blizzard outside or your name is Ernest Shackleton Jr.

AS RECENTLY AS a few hundred years ago, outerwear most commonly took the form of a cape or mantle, but the overcoat became an increasingly popular alternative as far back as the seventeenth century. It had its beginnings in the humble riding coat, a loose and purely functional garment worn by horsemen and soldiers. The heavy wool greatcoat evolved during the next two hundred years, influenced by military garb. When the world map was being chopped up during the Napoleonic era, for example, the coat was trimmed or lined in fur and decorated with braid and frog-fastenings for an exotic Eastern European look. In the U.S. around the time of the Civil War, it gained shoulder capes and overlapping collars like those on the winter greatcoats for Confederate and Union soldiers (who froze in the bitter cold, nevertheless).

THE LAST HALF of the nineteenth century was a golden age for men's dress overcoats, several bearing the names of the British aristocrats and places first associated with them. They include the Chesterfield, a slightly tapered coat, in either a single-breasted fly-front or double-breasted style, often with a velvet collar; the Raglan, a less formal, loose-fitting coat with full-cut sleeves and no shoulder seam; and the Ulster, a double-breasted long overcoat with a large convertible collar and a half or full belt.

THE ARMED SERVICES have bequeathed to us several topcoat perennials. The trench coat, a British army raincoat, emerged from the muddy battlefields of the First World War to become an evergreen classic. The navy popularized a pair of outerwear's most frequent phoenixes: the peacoat or reefer, a heavy double-breasted jacket in dark blue wool, was favored by nineteenth-century sailors and worn memorably by Jack Nicholson in the 1973 film *The Last Detail*; and the duffle coat, a three-quarter-length hooded sack fastened with leather loops and horn toggles, which was standard issue in the Royal Navy during the First World War. These days that coat comes in everything from tweed and camel hair to shearling and leather, fabrics that turn it into sophisticated casual wear that can be worn over a suit on less formal occasions.

PERHAPS THE MOST popular of all casual cold-weather cover-ups is the parka—or anorak, as its Inuit creators called it. Originally made of animal skins, it was a water-and-wind-resistant garment used for hunting and kayaking. The hooded jacket initially became fashionable in a gabardine shell version that skiers began wearing during the Depression, but it was Eddie Bauer, the Seattle sporting goods specialist, who invented the lightweight, quilted, down-filled parka, which he began manufacturing in 1936. In the 1950s, the U.S. military developed the nylon snorkel version, which had a hood that zipped snugly around the face.

OUTERWEAR IN GENERAL has made full use of improved weaving techniques and of the synthetic fibers that have developed since the first one, nylon, was invented just before the Second World War. Even luxury fabrics such as cashmere are sometimes combined with synthetics or treated with proprietary finishing processes—Teflon laminate, for instance—that waterproof them while leaving them breathable, so you don't get clammy. Because today's coats are lighter in weight and svelter than ever before, you can now keep warm without sacrificing style—or space in your overhead bag.

The Essential Topcoat

*Gone are the days of the bulky greatcoat. Today's coats convey stylish self-possession in a trim silhouette.
Here's what to look for in your dressiest, most important cold-weather garment.*

➤ THE COLLAR

A simple collar with a notched lapel is classy but unstuffy. A contrasting fabric collar—most often velvet, sometimes fur—is a hallmark of the dressier Chesterfield coat that's best for formal occasions and evening wear.

➤ THE SHOULDER

Not too wide, and go easy on the padding or you'll sprout superhero shoulders when you put the coat on over a suit. The overall effect should be crisp but natural.

➤ THE FABRIC

Navy cashmere is serious but not solemn. It's also light but warm enough for all but the most brutal weather. For that you'll need an overcoat, which is made of heavier wool or tweed—20- to 22-ounce cloth as opposed to a topcoat's 17–18 ounces. Camel hair is a snappier, less conventional—but still businesslike—alternative to classic dark cashmere.

➤ THE BUTTONS

Three buttons are the cleanest, most classic fastening arrangement. Four buttons create a higher—i.e., slightly more formal—gorge. A button-concealing placket is recommended for a sleeker, more minimalist look.

➤ THE FIT

The modern topcoat has a trim, close-to-the body silhouette. It should be the same size as your suit and not a size larger (always try it on over a tailored jacket). The sleeves of your jacket or shirt should never protrude beyond those of the coat.

➤ THE LENGTH

Keep it short—knee-length or just above—but not so brief that you start to look top-heavy. Below the knee is more traditional, especially for heavier coats like the polo (see p. 131), but can easily look dowdy. Ankle skimming is strictly for the frontier.

THE COAT: A ROSTER

THE CHESTERFIELD

Named after a well-to-do Regency dandy, the sixth earl of Chesterfield, this calf-length, single-breasted coat has always been a plutocratic kind of garment, thanks to a generally dark demeanor (navy, black, or dark gray) and its most distinctive element, a black velvet collar. This detail was reputedly inspired by late-eighteenth-century French noblemen who wore it to express sympathy silently and with style—for victims of the Reign of Terror.

THE TWEED COAT

In Scottish Gaelic, tweed was called *an clò mòr*, or "the big cloth." When it comes to tweeds, you can get away with a bolder pattern in a coat than you ever could in a suit—as long as you don't layer check over check. A true Prince of Wales check, for example, is a modern classic: large-scale, in shades of red-brown and slate-gray. Cheviot tweed, made from the thick yarn of Cheviot sheep, is a sturdier weave suitable for rough-looking winter overcoats. With a tweed coat, keep the rest of your ensemble low-key and let the coat do all the talking.

Wear it to:
An inaugural ball.

Wear it to:
A book launch party.

OF CLASSIC OPTIONS

THE POLO COAT

From the early twentieth century until well after the Second World War, the polo coat was the all-enveloping outdoor equivalent of the bathrobe, donned by sportsmen to prevent a chill after sweating in the saddle or on the tennis court. Characterized by its roomy double-breasted cut, big, lumpy patch pockets, and a full or half belt, it is habitually made of a thick plush wool or camel hair to give instant warmth after the melee. Its enduring, vaguely gangsterish appeal—especially in the natural camel color—still has its modern devotees in America.

THE DUFFLE COAT

The good people of Duffel, Belgium, have been weaving thick, double-faced wool for centuries, but it wasn't until the Royal Navy adopted coats made from the fabric in the early twentieth century that the tiny village was put on the proverbial map. Then as now, these warm but relatively light coats had a capacious hood (which could be worn over a rigid cap) and four horn toggles down the front. Huge numbers of duffles were later sold as military surplus after the Second World War, thus paving the way for their present ubiquity.

THE PEACOAT

You'd be hard-pressed to find any fashion brand that doesn't offer some variation on the peacoat, the double-breasted wool coat with broad lapels and wooden buttons. That's only fitting, considering its global reach. Peacoats have been worn since the eighteenth century by European (and, later, American) sailors of all ranks and classes—"pea" derives from the Dutch word *pij*, the preferred type of cloth for early versions—and like the men who wore them, they went around the world and left their influence everywhere they went.

Wear it to:
A Harvard-Yale tailgate party.

Wear it to:
Sunday brunch.

Wear it to:
A loft party.

How to Wear a Coat

A man needs but three coats. Here's how to wear 'em.

WHETHER YOU'RE MAKING snowmen, desperately trying to keep your suit dry on an evening out, or navigating the winds blowing between the office and the parking garage, a good coat is indispensable. Your choices will boil down to the three types below.

THE PARKA	THE EVERYDAY	THE FORMAL
The classic parka comes in many guises these days. It's best with jeans and casual wear, but it can work with a suit. Just make sure that it's longer than your suit jacket, and streamlined. If you need to wear it to the office on a regular basis, a color other than bright orange or red will be more versatile. **Don't forget**: Limit the logos, chunky exterior zippers, and endless Velcro tabs.	For most days, you need a coat that multitasks, one that can segue from the office to, say, a ball game. Try one in a blend of cashmere and technical fabric that makes the jacket feel luxurious but keeps wind and water out. A fly front (where the buttons are hidden) suggests higher quality. **Don't forget**: Light-color coats show dirt quickly. Be sure yours is cleaned regularly.	When dressing up, a simple single-breasted coat in dark wool (cashmere if you can) will always make the grade. Make sure the coat fits over your suit (have a jacket on when you try it) but don't get too big, lest it look borrowed. The waist should be slightly suppressed—you don't want to look like you're wearing a bathrobe. **Don't forget**: Use a lint brush before you leave the house.

NEIL YOUNG AND THE PEACOAT

➥ *Sailors have worn a version of the peacoat for centuries, but in 1969, Canadian rock legend Neil Young paired his with a corduroy button-down and a black turtleneck and invested the salty jacket with folksy earnestness. The versatile coat has other moods: Matinee idol John Barrymore embodied Melvillean romanticism in the 1930 movie* Moby Dick.

PETER FONDA AND THE LEATHER JACKET

➥ *In the 1969 road movie* Easy Rider, *Peter Fonda's leather jacket, a close-fitting European style emblazoned with Old Glory, is as fine an emblem of the rebellious idealism of the period as the movie's rock soundtrack. A decade later, pierced and deconstructed, the motorcycle jacket became a symbol of British punk rock, and Sid Vicious reportedly wished to be buried in his. Even on art-world eminence Richard Serra, a black leather jacket conveys a tinge of black-sheep individualism.*

{ *The* CLASSICS }
The Leather Motorcycle Jacket

THE PERFECTO MOTORCYCLE JACKET was already a quarter century old when Marlon Brando immortalized it in the 1954 biker flick *The Wild One*. The original dates from 1928, when a Harley-Davidson distributor asked Schott Bros., a Staten Island outerwear manufacturer, to create a leather motorcycle jacket. (The brothers had long branded their raincoats under the name Perfecto, after one of the founders' favorite cigar.) The new jacket was rugged enough to protect a speeding rider from the elements (and the blacktop, should he crash), with a zipper and belted waist to keep out the wind. Schott also designed and produced the leather bomber jacket for the Army Air Corps during the Second World War. Though returning veterans turned the bomber into another civilian menswear staple, it has never quite attained the Perfecto's iconic status, let alone its subversive edge. It has been the ultimate badge of bad-boy cool ever since, worn by such stylish renegades as James Dean, Jim Morrison, Lou Reed, Bruce Springsteen, and Johnny Depp.

A Few Things You Didn't Know About
SHEARLING

Long the requisite territory of mountain men and men on the outer edges of style, shearling can't be beat for its utility and look. There is nothing warmer in winter months and, when it's combined with modern lines, no more stylish alternative for surviving the cold. And it's just damn comfortable.

1} SHEARLING PREDATES FASHION.
It's believed that Neanderthals invented the practice of using animal skins as clothing to protect themselves against cold European climates. In 1995, Russian scientists discovered a frozen Scythian warrior in a burial mound on the Siberian steppes.

2} IT DOESN'T GROW ON TREES.
To make shearling, hides from yearling lambs are tanned with the wool still attached. It's then trimmed to an even length, usually about a half inch.

3} WOOL IS THE OLDEST HIGH-TECH FIBER.
It's durable and stays comfortable over a wide range of temperatures. It's also incredibly light. As a bonus, it stays warm when wet and dries off quickly—and doesn't easily pick up body odor.

4} YOU'RE NOT JUMPING OUT OF PLANES WEARING IT, BUT YOU COULD.
The original sheepskin bomber jacket was designed in England in 1926 by a former stuntman from America named Leslie Irvin. He went on to supply parachutes to the Allies during the Second World War, and gave his name to the sheepskin flying jackets that his company produced for Allied bomber crews.

The Summer Raincoat

And other lightweight solutions to freak storms, chilly nights, hyperactive air-conditioning, and assorted seasonal hazards

THE RAIN-COAT	THE GOLF JACKET	THE WINDBREAKER	THE WEEK-ENDER
Wear a standard lined trench coat in the middle of August and you'll sweat straight through your shirt. Opt for an unlined coat that shields you from the elements without weighing you down.	Stave off the chill of early-morning tee times (or other sporting events) with a close-fitting cotton jacket. Look for wider armholes that maximize movement.	A grown man has no business in a poncho, but a zip-up nylon windbreaker allows you to weather the fiercest of storms without compromising your style.	For protection against sub-arctic air-conditioning and increasingly chilly nights, an unlined, all-cotton weekend jacket helps ease the transition to early autumn.

*** THE (STYLE) HISTORY: WATERPROOF FABRICS ***

FOR A LONG TIME, they were either functionally nonporous (like rubber) or actively water-repellent (like waxed cotton). But since these coatings work well only on tightly woven synthetic fabrics, designers could only make stuff that looked more functional than fashionable. Gore-Tex, invented in the 1970s, allowed your sweat out and kept rain from getting in, but it's only ever been used in sport clothing. Recent advances have changed everything. Coating wool with high-tech hydrophobic substances adds wet-weather protection yet allows a luxurious wool suit to look luxurious.

INSPECTOR CLOUSEAU AND THE TRENCH COAT

➤ As the comically inept Inspector Clouseau of the Pink Panther movies, Peter Sellers wore his trench coat buttoned and belted, an attempt to preserve a semblance of suave control as Clouseau bumbled through crime scenes. James Coburn played down the official associations of the khaki trench by wearing it open over a black turtleneck, while German artist and intellectual Joseph Beuys teamed it with his signature outfit: jeans, felt hat, and fishing vest.

WHAT YOU NEED TO KNOW ABOUT

The System of Down

Buying a parka suited for the white-collar world

GOOSE DOWN

Fluffy, natural, and sustainable, it's still the best insulation in terms of warmth-to-weight ratio, compressibility, and longevity. Performance is expressed as "fill power," the number of cubic inches an ounce of down occupies, which ranges from 450 (adequate), to 650 (good), to 850 (superlative). The first is more than sufficient for a cold day's stroll in the park; the last will keep you toasty on the summit of K2.

SYNTHETIC DOWN

Goose down loses its insulating properties when it gets wet, and it takes a long time to dry. A good synthetic down like PrimaLoft, which is fluffy like the natural stuff though not as light, will keep you warm even when waterlogged. It's what you need in pouring rain.

FABRICS

The ideal parka shell needs to be water-resistant, windproof, breathable, and down-impermeable. Which means you're best off with synthetic fabrics—nylon, polyester, and laminates such as Gore-Tex or Dry-Loft. Generally, the more weather resistant the material, the heavier and costlier it will be. In better jackets, all seams are sealed with protective tape for additional waterproofing.

CONSTRUCTION

In sewn-through or quilted construction, the parka's shell and liner are stitched together to hold the down in place. Although this technique creates cold areas along the lines of stitching, it's adequate for use around town. Baffled construction, in which the down is held in compartments between the shell and the liner, is bulkier and more expensive but much warmer. Don't hit Everest without it.

CLEANING

Dry-cleaning chemicals not only strip the goose down of its natural oils, causing it to break up, but also can damage certain synthetic shell fabrics. Jackets should be laundered in a front-loading washing machine (agitators can rip the shell), using the gentle cycle with warm water and a down-specific detergent. Tumble dry the garment thoroughly at a low heat with two or three tennis balls tossed in to fluff up the down.

STORING

For long-term storage, keep down jackets, loosely folded or on hangers, in breathable cotton or paper bags (never use plastic). Avoid compressing them—it will reduce the down's warmth-giving loft. In the closet, hanging your jacket upside-down will prevent the down from bunching along the bottom hem.

{ *The RULES* }

•

WEARING A TRASH-BAG PONCHO is actually worse than getting wet.

WEARING WET DOWN IS LIKE WEARING OATMEAL— be sure you have a waterproof shell or a good umbrella.

HOW LAYERS WORK

Warmth from the inside out

(**A**) INNER LAYER ⟶ (**B**) MIDDLE LAYERS ⟶ (**C**) OUTER LAYER

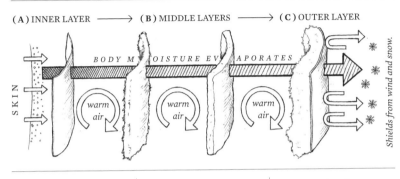

{ A }	{ B }	{ C }
Silk, polypropylene, or another nonabsorbent material draws moisture away from the skin.	*Wool, fleece, or another insulating material traps warm air between layers and transfers moisture from one layer to the next.*	*Gore-Tex, gabardine, or another breathable material lets body moisture escape while staving off wind and water.*

Down: the Facts

Since being invented in the 1930s and 1940s, wind- and water-resistant materials like nylon and polyester have been essential for the outdoors. When stuffed with down, they have become the ultrawarm garments that have helped make extreme mountaineering possible. Here, a few facts:

1} Each cluster of goose down contains dozens of filaments that trap warm air.

2} Its insulating ability is measured in "loft," the number of cubic inches an ounce of down fills. Good stuff fills 650; the best, 850.

3} The top down comes from Eastern Europe— and from the Hutterites, spiritual cousins of the Amish, from the northern Great Plains.

4} On rainy days, you're better off with wool or a synthetic insulation like PrimaLoft.

....

The **SARTORIAL CANON**

⋙ • ⋘

The Coat and Other Outerwear

....

BARBOUR ➤ For more than a century, English aristocrats donned outerwear from J. Barbour & Sons, a family-owned company in the north of England that produces "clothes for country pursuits." Many Americans have been attracted to the Beaufort, a genderless waxed-canvas jacket with a corduroy collar. www.barbour.com

BERETTA ➤ The Beretta family of Lombardy, Italy, has been making guns since the sixteenth century. Today it also produces a wide range of stylish, technically advanced outerwear for use in upland, waterfowl, and big-game hunting. The company recently launched the youthful 1526 line, which includes cotton and steel-fiber goose-down jackets, stretch corduroy chinos, and cotton and nylon field jackets. www.beretta.com

MONCLER ➤ Founded in France in 1952, Moncler produced remarkably light, down-filled ski jackets that became a fashion craze with Milanese teenagers in the 1980s. An Italian entrepreneur took over the brand and successfully reinvented the puffy-yet-sleek jackets as stylish urban wear. By the mid-2000s, the Moncler parka, previously unknown in America, had become synonymous with the down coat. www.moncler.com

VICTORINOX ➤ The makers of the Swiss Army knife also produce Victorinox outerwear, just as thoughtfully designed, painstakingly made, and ruggedly constructed as its ubiquitous pocket knife. Victorinox offers lightweight sailing jackets, trench coats, and down-filled parkas with trim fits and breathable fabrics. www.swissarmy.com

WOOLRICH ➤ Venerable American mill Woolrich was established in 1832 by a traveling salesman selling rugged goods to loggers. Its red-and-black plaid barn coats, lumberjack jackets, and blankets are the real McCoy. Recently, Woolrich hired a young Japanese designer, Daiki Suzuki, to design a contemporary urban line using the mill's traditional fabrics. www.woolrich.com

ACCESSORIES HAVE ANOTHER great thing going for them: they pack a big bang for the buck. You may not be in the four-figure-suit league, but add a pair of good $100 cuff links to a white French-cuffed shirt, pair it with your jeans, and you'll get a tenfold return on the way you look and feel.

TAKE THE NECKTIE as an example. When Steve Case, the CEO of AOL, and Gerald Levin, his elder-statesman counterpart at Time Warner, announced the merger of the two corporations in 2000, the younger man from the new dot-com world wore a tie, but the heavyweight corporate titan did not. Levin's attempt at hipness backfired; it was Case who looked disconcertingly cool and modern. A decade later, although the necktie is as firmly tucked under the boardroom chin as ever, a surprising number of twenty- and thirtysomethings are choosing to emulate Case and cover their throats. In liberating the necktie from the corporate straightjacket (often by means of acid colors, or patterns just slightly *off*), these sartorially aware young guns are acknowledging its power and practicality: the tie holds your shirt collar neatly in place, preventing it from sagging or becoming misshapen.

YOU MIGHT BE INCLINED, as are many men, to overlook the pocket square, the necktie's city-slicker cousin, as a lightweight—slightly effete and not for the average guy. With all due respect, you'd be mistaken. The pocket square more than pulls its sartorial weight, adding a punch of color to a drab ensemble, a razor-sharp slice of white-linen elegance to a navy suit, or, if the occasion is right, replacing a necktie altogether.

MOST OF US PROBABLY have far more ties than wristwatches—the watch being a particularly potent and often extravagant status symbol. Judging by the mind-boggling range of brands, the celebrity endorsements, and the latent heirloom potential in a watch, selecting and purchasing one can amount to a research project. The earliest watches first appeared in Germany at the end of the fifteenth century; they were spherical, ruinously expensive pieces of jewelry worn on a chain around the neck. Wristwatches were introduced before the First World War but became widely popular only in the 1920s, replacing the pocket watch almost entirely by the end of the Second World War. With the exception of Flavor Flav, most men haven't yet returned to favoring gaudy chronometers around their necks, but a wristwatch, the only piece of jewelry most men wear, is almost as visible and expressive as a tie. You might want to avoid both the wafer-thin and flashy types; plain and elegant should be your watchwords.

AS IT SHOULD be with your cuff links. If you must wear gemstones, only do so with black tie, and even then they shouldn't be bigger than your thumbnail—the cuff links, that is, not the stones. It's also perfectly stylish to sport unadorned gold or silver ovals or rectangles; in fact, such simplicity is preferable if the cuff links comprise two elements joined by a chain, one for either side of the cuff. But the real point of using cuff links is not display but the fact that they allow you the grown-up privilege of wearing French cuffs.

SOME MEN THINK wearing a formal hat is grown-up, too. Emblematic, as opposed to purely protective, male headwear dates back to thirteenth-century linen bonnets that tied under the chin. For the next seven hundred years, a gentleman would no more go outdoors hatless than he would shoeless; what he wore on his head was a vital expression of his social position and personal character. Then, in the 1960s, the venerable hat rule was unceremoniously abolished, and men largely gave up their elegant fedoras, crisp homburgs, and soft trilbies as if they were health hazards. In case you haven't noticed, hats are back on the heads of smartly dressed hipsters and businessmen, in the traditional forms mentioned above—but now with a distinctly twenty-first-century spin in terms of materials, styling, and trim.

ACCESSORIES

Whether purely practical or outright embellishment, accessories are where conformity leaves off and individual expression begins. The right ones will bring your wardrobe into sharp focus.

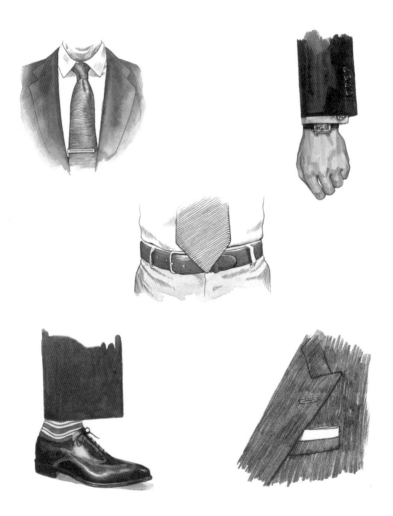

➡ TIE

The necktie can still be the most expressive piece of cloth in a man's wardrobe. Consider pattern, width (the wider the tie, the bolder you'll look), fabric (sumptuous silk is still the gold standard), and fold (see pp. 148–51).

➡ SILK POCKET SQUARE

Much more than a quaint remnant from your grandfather's day, this diminutive square of fine silk, cotton, or linen—depending on the season and occasion—packs a formidable style punch. Every man should have at least one. Use it (see p. 152).

➡ CUFF LINKS

Worn with French cuff shirts, cuff links serve an obvious purpose. But they also add formality, polish, and—chosen well—subtle wit (see p. 153).

➡ WATCH

A good timepiece says as much about your status as your shoes. Oh yeah, and it tells time (see pp. 154–58).

➡ WALLET

For credit cards only—cash goes in a money clip in your front pocket. A good wallet is not just a place to keep your stuff; it's a source of personal satisfaction.

➡ SUNGLASSES

Once worn routinely only for outdoor sports and in sunny places with beautiful people, sunglasses are now considered an essential weapon in UV protection. It's just a bonus that they look so frickin' cool (see pp. 159–61).

➡ LEATHER GLOVES

Choose cashmere-lined supple calf or deerskin for dress; tougher wool-lined cowhide for weekend snowball fights. Throw in a pair of driving gloves if you're so inclined (see p. 163).

➡ CASHMERE SCARF

Nothing keeps you warmer or feels better against your skin—or someone else's—than cashmere. Try a bright color or subdued pattern that contrasts with your overcoat.

➡ LEATHER BELT

Simple elegance is best when choosing a belt. Buckles the size of your wallet and over-the-top hand-tooling are best worn to the rodeo. And don't make the biggest mistake: not wearing one at all. You're not fully dressed without one.

➡ SOCKS

It's hard to get excited about socks, but they're an overlooked opportunity to add a splash of color to a monochromatic ensemble. Your best choice for quality: merino wool in winter and pima cotton in summer.

THE TIE

A History

Q *I've always heard that the necktie started as something to wipe your face with, sort of a napkin around the neck. True?*
No—you're thinking of the jockstrap, first used by ancient Greeks as an olive-oil strainer. The origins of knotted neckwear appear to be military: Chinese statues of warriors dating from the third century B.C. show them wearing scarves, apparently as protection from crappy weather. The fabric noose we call a necktie derives more directly from a visit to Paris in about 1660 by a crack military regiment from Croatia. King Louis XIV was so wowed by the brightly colored silk neckerchiefs worn by the Croatian officers that in keeping with the French gift for slavish idiocracy, he appropriated the Croat motif as an insignia of royalty and created his own regiment, known as the Royal Cravattes. *Cravate*, of course, is French for Croatian—just as *fop* is English for Frenchman. In many countries, using your tie as a napkin is grounds for criminal prosecution and/or deportation. Here's a tip: stick it in your shirt when eating.

A WELL-TIED TIE
IS THE FIRST SERIOUS
STEP IN LIFE.

—*Oscar Wilde*

The Repp Tie

You'd be forgiven for assuming the repp is a homegrown American classic like the chino or the penny loafer—its preppie pedigree is as solid as the rocks in a gin and tonic. But the repp originated across the pond, like the trench coat, in the nineteenth century. The British gentry used ties with stripes in strictly prescribed colors and widths to signal the schools, clubs, and regiments they belonged to. During the First World War, the future Duke of Windsor turned the handsome blue-and-red broad-striped tie of his elite Grenadier Guards regiment into a natty fashion accessory that Americans then adopted wholesale. In 1920, Brooks Brothers made a concession to outraged British sensibilities when they ran the diagonal stripes down from right to left, the opposite direction from traditional club and regimental ties. (Today you'll see both configurations.) Stripped of its upstairs–downstairs connotations, the striped repp tie quickly became an American staple, at home in boardrooms and classrooms alike. Of late the repp has been reborn in a narrow-cut, irony-laced guise that sweeps away any lingering old-school mustiness. Paired with a skinny suit or dark jeans, it signals American attitude at its best.

Knots: A How-to

FOUR-IN-HAND

This is the move your dad taught you. Five quick motions and you're done. An easy pinch in the middle gives you a centered dimple. And the skinny knot works well with a button-down.

HALF WINDSOR

Adding a couple of extra moves widens the knot, which works with most collars, and it should be wide enough to fill the center space of your collar.

WINDSOR

Named for the Duke of Windsor, perfected by Frank Sinatra, this is the grand-daddy of knots. It take a little work, yes, but the results will leave others asking how you pulled it off. And with a knot this fat, only a wide, spread collar will do.

THE BOW TIE

Every man should know how to do this

1. Make a simple knot with both ends, allowing slightly more length (one or two inches) on the end of A.

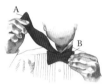

2. Lift A out of the way, fold B into the normal bow shape, and position it on the first knot you made.

3. Drop A vertically over folded end B.

4. Then double A back on itself and position it over the knot so that the two folded ends make a cross.

5. The hard part: Pass folded end A under and behind the left side (yours) of the knot, and through the loop behind folded end B.

6. Tighten the knot you have created, straightening any crumples and creases, particularly in the narrow part at the center.

CHARLES EAMES AND THE BOW TIE

➡ *The bow tie: for college professors and good ol' boys, right? Charles Eames—with his wife, Ray, the alpha and omega of modern American design—didn't think so. In fact, he never wore anything else around his neck, except a bandanna in the great outdoors. (That we won't recommend—unless you're one of the Village People.) Eames understood that the avant-garde doesn't break from tradition but evolves from it. The Cat in the Hat, another adventurous— nay, mischievous—figure of the same era, sported his red bow tie with floppy abandon.*

IN THE JEANS-AND-A-SUIT-JACKET ENVIRONMENT,

A POCKET SQUARE CAN STAND IN FOR A TIE

HERE'S HOW:

Astaire	**Churchill**	**JFK**	**Bond, James**
To be done only with a silk handkerchief. Begin by spreading the material across a flat surface and pinching at the center, allowing the fabric to pillow around the pinch. Only an elegant pattern will do.	Constructed in the same fashion as the Astaire pocket square but with the additional step of folding up the corners. This style is slightly more ragged in a very purposeful way. Must still be done with silk.	The structured nature of this style can be done with almost any material: silk, linen, or cotton. Very measured and exact, it calls for a quiet pattern on the hankie and is usually worn by men you'd trust to invest your money.	Straight out of the 1960s comes this straight-across approach. Donned by spies, news anchors, and heads of state, this style is simple and clean. It should be done with a white linen or cotton handkerchief.

It's easy to dismiss pocket squares as trendy and just a little bit twee, but the fact is that a certain kind of man—the well-dressed kind—has always had one at the ready to complement or even sub in for a necktie. • **Color:** White goes with everything, of course, but for one that stands out and ages extraordinarily well, start with a silk square in a dark shade, or one that highlights a single color in your tie or shirt. Choose by trial and error or enlist the help of an adept salesperson. Match the material exactly to your tie and you'll be taken outside, a bucket will be placed over your head, and you'll be beaten with sticks. • **Fold:** Fold it with points or straight across, or pinch it in the center and stuff the point into your breast pocket for a slightly jauntier look. The banker's straight edge (see Bond, James, above) should be sharp enough that you could shave with it. Press in those creases as you fold. Because the breast-pocket edge of a suit is generally cut on the slant, your pocket square may not line up when you place it in the pocket. Our advice: cheat. Use a safety pin to hold the square in place.

THE COUP DE GRÂCE: A POCKET SQUARE

THE WELL-CHOSEN LINK:
Mark of a Professional

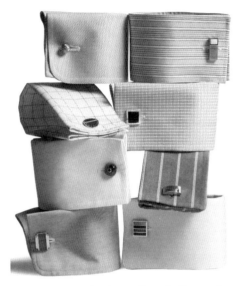

IN THE MODERN business-formal climate, the French cuff and its attendant cuff link are the markers of professionalism. A well-chosen link will say as much about you across a conference room as a watch. Or a pocket square. The options are vast, so observe a few ground rules:

1. If you need just one all-purpose pair, simple silver disks or squares are classic and appropriate for any occasion.

2. Colored links should match a color in your tie or shirt. Avoid clashing patterns on links and cuffs.

3. Wear novelty links (typewriter keys, working miniature clocks) at your own risk.

A HIERARCHY OF CUFF LINKS

Use this handy guide to sort your cuff links into convenient piles.

The Silk Knot
Often free with shirts, they don't last long, but they add color. Not for evening.

The Bar and Rocker
The most common form of cuff link and the easiest to clasp.

The Barbell
Uses a lot of metal, giving weight to a cuff.

The Chain Link
The most elegant. And the most tricky.

GIANNI AGNELLI AND THE WRISTWATCH

➥ *Time is money, and nothing says "don't waste mine" like wearing your molto elegante wristwatch for the world to see. Italian mogul Gianni Agnelli's style statement was an instance of fashion following function. The Fiat heir preferred his barrel cuffs so snug that he had to wear his luxury watch over his cuff. Al Gore's bulky digital timepiece, on the other hand, conveys the pragmatic nature of a seasoned politician who's presumably keeping his eye on the public's time and money.*

FOR EVERY OCCASION, THERE IS THE RIGHT TICKER

How to Wear a Watch

There are some timepieces that fit all occasions. But they are rare. Very rare. Much more likely is the scenario in which the watch on your wrist must change with the appointment in your schedule.

FOR HIGH ROLLIN'

Black-tie and other expressly formal events call for a discreet and elegant watch that is small in diameter and slim enough to slip in and out of a French cuff. In this scenario, always match the color of your cuff links to the metal of your watch. If the links are enamel or set with stones, go one better and match the stone of the link to the dial color of the watch's face.

FOR LOUNGIN'

Hang time calls for a big watch to dress up your casual clothes, whether you're in a T-shirt or tweed. Look for a watch in less dressy-looking brushed steel with a chunky body and an interesting face. Bonus points here if the watch's pedigree derives from aviation, sailing, or car racing.

FOR WORKIN'

A chunky chronograph in steel or yellow gold makes a bold statement across a conference table. Only you can decide how flashy you should go, but remember to match the links.

FOR SWEATIN'

You may have a gutsy, top-of-the-line steel chronograph from a great Swiss maker. It may have a host of macho functions, but be sensible and leave it at home. The smart choice here is a durable rubber sports watch that can take a beating. It was made to get twisted and scratched. That fancy metal hardware was not.

{ *The RULES* }

•

DIAMOND-ENCRUSTED WATCHES ARE ONLY for pimps, hip-hop moguls, and heiresses.

•

PEOPLE WHO WEAR DIAMOND-ENCRUSTED watches never know what time it is.

•

A WATCH SHOULD BE WORN SECURELY on your wrist. It is not a bracelet.

•

THERE IS A DIFFERENCE BETWEEN water-resistant and waterproof. This is usually learned the hard way.

•

SLEEK WATCHES ON LEATHER STRAPS LOOK BEST FOR dressing up, and heavier metal-link bands go better with casual clothing.

THE DAYS OF THE DIGITAL WATCH ARE NUMBERED.

—*Tom Stoppard*

Close-up on Luxury Watches

Seven important questions to ask yourself before you go out and drop big coin

Tourbillion

Invented two hundred years ago, the elite mechanism corrects for gravity.

Rotor

In a self-winding mechanical watch, it spins in response to the wearer's wrist movements

Moon Phase

An example of a complicated function in a mechanical watch.

1. SPLURGE OR NOT?

Luxury watches range from under $1,000 to $100,000 and more. Among the most expensive are the prized tourbillions, which only an elite group of master watchmakers has the skills to produce. (The two-hundred-year-old mechanism consists of a revolving carriage that holds the balance wheel and escapement and makes a complete turn every sixty seconds to average out timekeeping errors caused by gravity.) Ultimately, a watch is a status symbol.

2. ROSE, WHITE, OR YELLOW GOLD?

The tint of a piece of gold depends on the proportion of copper and silver mixed with the pure gold. Yellow will always be stylish, but you might consider one of the myriad rose-gold options. Rose has the most copper of the three golds, which gives it a soft, pinkish hue.

3. STEEL OR TITANIUM?

High-grade stainless steel is strong, shiny, and highly resistant to rust and corrosion. But titanium is 30 percent stronger and 50 percent lighter than steel, more corrosion resistant, antimagnetic, and even hypoallergenic. A titanium watch does feel amazingly light and comfortable on the wrist, but the trade-off is a subdued—some say dull—gray watch that, for all its strength, scratches easily.

4. SIMPLE OR COMPLICATED?

In watchmaking terms, a complication is any function beyond simple time telling in a mechanical watch, such as a calendar or a moon-phase indicator. Usually, though, the term refers to sophisticated mechanisms like perpetual calendars and split-second chronographs, which contain hundreds of tiny hand-assembled parts. because they're so labor-intensive, complicated watches are expensive and prized for the feats they perform.

5. BIG OR BIGGER?

Men's wristwatches have grown as if on steroids; they broke the forty-millimeter-diameter barrier at the turn of this century. The reason? Mostly style. The trend was largely inspired by the reissue of an old Italian diver's watch, which was originally designed large so it would be visible in the murky Mediterranean. If your watch looks like a hockey puck on your wrist, you're either horologically chic or showy, depending on the season.

6. DO I NEED A CHRONOGRAPH?

Most guys prize chronographs—timepieces with a stopwatch function—thanks to the macho, sporty look of all those buttons and subdials. They are also functional and can time an event to one-fifth of a second for mechanical chronos and to one-hundredth of a second in digital quartz chronos. But unless you've just signed up for the Ironman, they're mostly for adornment.

7. WATER RESISTANCE: FIVE BARS OR TWENTY?

Watches have different levels of water resistance, indicated on the dial or case back. Pay close attention to the fine print, because the depth units are anything but universal. Most companies give water resistance in meters. Occasionally you'll come across ATMs (for atmospheres) or bars, both of which are equal to ten meters. Once you've done the math, choose a depth based on your needs. Water-resistant to fifty meters means you can wear it in the shower. Sports watches generally have hundred-meter (swimming, snorkeling) or two-hundred-meter (recreational scuba diving) water resistance. You don't need more than that unless you intend to wear the watch while deep-sea diving.

A GUIDE TO
WATCH CARE

Get your mechanical watch serviced at a good repair shop every few years. Professionals will strip down the movement, clean it with ultrasound equipment, oil the works, tighten or change the waterproof joints, and polish the case. Find an authorized shop through your brand's Web site.

· ·

Avoid exposing your watch to extreme heat or cold. That means removing it before entering saunas or snowball fights or meeting Ann Coulter.

· ·

Watches with leather straps shouldn't be worn every day. They need to be aired out between wears so that the leather can dry.

· ·

Change the battery on your quartz watch every three years. Ignore this benchmark and your battery could start leaking acid, corroding the interior of your watch. Then it will no longer work.

· ·

Even if your watch is self-winding, wind it once every few weeks to keep the wheels in motion and the oils fluid.

· ·

There is nothing wrong with a watch that can be cured by shaking the hell out of it.

Mechanical vs. Quartz

KNOW THE DIFFERENCE

MECHANICAL ➤ A timepiece whose movement is powered by a mainspring connected to a system of gears, wheels, and weights. The hands of mechanical watches move smoothly around the face. However, because of the high number of moving parts, they gain or lose a few seconds per day and about one hour per year in accuracy. Mechanical watches involve a high degree of crafts-manship and inhabit the upper echelons of watchmaking.

QUARTZ ➤ Unlike a mechanical watch, a quartz watch has fewer moving parts and is regulated by an electrified sliver of quartz, which vibrates at a constant rate when charged. It is inexpensive to make and exceedingly accu-rate, losing on average only one minute of accuracy per year. A quartz movement can be identified immediately by following the movement of the watch's hands, which jump from second to second instead of sweeping fluidly like those of mechanical watches.

{ *The* CLASSICS }
The Omega Speedmaster

FOR A SWISS WATCH, THE SPEEDMASTER is a peculiarly American success story. The Omega Speedmaster Professional Chronograph debuted in 1957 and was selected by NASA technicians in 1965 as the only watch flight-qualified for all manned space missions. It has graced the wrists of every Apollo crew member from then on. It was the first watch worn on the moon during the Apollo 11 mission—thus earning its nickname, Moon Watch (the original stainless-steel band was replaced with Velcro to enable it to fit over the sleeve of a space suit). Its moment of true glory came in 1970, when its consistent timekeeping saved the lives of the crew of Apollo 13, including Jim Lovell, who used its chronograph functions to time the firing of the secondary rockets that manhandled the disabled spacecraft through reentry. With its movie-star looks—classic stainless steel case, black face, and three interior dials—the Speedmaster has won cameo roles in films ranging from *The Right Stuff* to *The Corruptor*, with Hong-Kong star Chow Yun-Fat.

{ *The* CLASSICS }

The Ray-Ban Wayfarer

BY 1983, WHEN TOM CRUISE wore his in *Risky Business*, the Ray-Ban Wayfarer already meant West Coast cool. Derived from a smaller, leaner 1950s original, Cruise's screen frames embodied the swaggering, top-down prosperity of the decade. Ray-Ban's original wire-framed Aviator, adopted by the air force during the Second World War and famously worn by General MacArthur, still gets the long-term plaudits from style gurus, but the Wayfarer, more deeply suffused with Hollywood meaning, deserves the cooler props. It was designed in 1952 by inventor Raymond Stegeman, whose patent drawing reveals the original Wayfarer in a decidedly goofier, cat-glasses shape typical of 1950s design. By 1961, when Audrey Hepburn wore a pair in *Breakfast at Tiffany's*, the frames had grown into their trademark silhouette, generously proportioned yet streamlined. Since then, film and rock stars from Bob Dylan to Roy Orbison, Jack Nicholson, and Elvis Costello have embraced the Wayfarer as a signature accessory—or a perfect disguise.

You've Got Nowhere to Put Your

SUNGLASSES

{ OPTION 1 }

Don't rotate them upward so they're sitting on top of your head. Instead, make sure the protective case that came with your sunglasses is always in your brief-case or workbag. Get in the habit of using it.

{ OPTION 2 }

No briefcase? If you're wearing a suit or a jacket, put your sunglasses in your top inside pocket, with the lenses facing out for optimal protection. Stowing in any other pocket increases the risk of frame damage or lens scratching.

{ OPTION 3 }

No jacket? Lay the glasses on the table, lenses up. Admire them occasionally. Do not forget them when you get up to leave.

{ *The* RULES }

•

YOU SHOULD TAKE YOUR SHADES OFF *when speaking to someone who's not wearing any. It's a trust issue.*

YOUR EYEGLASSES
Should Contrast, Not Mimic, The Shape Of Your Face. Here's a quick guide:

YOUR SHAPE: Heart
YOUR SPECS: A heart-shaped face already has a lot of definition. Since your head is top-heavy, go for a geometric frame that gives some width to the lower half of your face.

YOUR SHAPE: Square
YOUR SPECS: Since a square face already has angles, go for a round or oval frame that shapes your cheekbones. A decorative frame with width will often do the trick.

YOUR SHAPE: Round
YOUR SPECS: Avoid dark frames; they only make your face appear heavy. A round face needs direction, so opt for angular and narrow frames—never a square or a circle.

YOUR SHAPE: Oval
YOUR SPECS: A modern rectangle is best for an oval face. Because your face is longer than it is wide, you'll need frames that provide width. If your face is wider than it is long, go the opposite way.

TOM CRUISE AND THE SIGNATURE SUNGLASSES

➡ *In 1983's* Risky Business, *Tom Cruise was a teenage dork before he discovered the power of a pair of Ray-Ban Wayfarers. That year, 360,000 pairs of the famous shades were sold, up from only 18,000 in 1981—a fact that speaks to the magic of product placement and a star in Ray-Bans. As the Blues Brothers, John Belushi and Dan Ackroyd began wearing Wayfarers in 1978, channeling the look of blues legends like John Lee Hooker and Ray Charles.*

ANDRÉ 3000 AND THE EXTRA 10 PERCENT
➡ *André is the modern dandy* par excellence, *with an eye for telling sartorial details that pull everything together—like a diamond-pane silk scarf that mediates between a tweed herringbone jacket and a mono-chrome turtleneck. Even if you never dress remotely like him, you could do worse than follow his example of reining in flamboyant color and old-school preppy by pairing them with classic tailoring. His key is that he's always in charge. Which is precisely where you should be, even if all you're into is a three-button suit.*

THE HAND THAT ROCKS
Four steps to insulating your fingers

 Your hand's size is measured from its circumference at the knuckles. Find out what it is, and buy accordingly.

 The inside is as important as the outside. Look for a knitted cashmere lining.

 Gloves don't have to match your clothes but should at least complement your wardrobe. Black and brown are the most versatile choices.

 Leather needs care if it's going to last. If gloves get wet, don't dry them on a heater, which would dessicate the leather.

A CELEBRATION OF UTTER UTILITY
Boiled-wool mittens

YOU PROBABLY TRADED your mittens for gloves when you turned ten and never looked back. Good for you. But as any polar explorer with ten fingers can tell you, boiled-wool mittens are among the simplest and most effective ways of shielding your hands from the cold. The best kinds are made from pure knit wool that's been boiled to create a dense, feltlike fabric that insulates better than most other untreated woods or leathers. They're tough, naturally water-resistant, and all but windproof, and because wool "breathes" and releases moisture, heat-sapping sweat won't build up on your hands. No cutting-edge fabrics. No twenty-first-century bells and whistles. Just wool and hot water. But for those long waits on the train platform or the triple-overtime nail-biter at Lambeau, there's nothing warmer.

The Way of the
SCARF

The Novice
A rakish wrap that warms the neck and the sternum.

The Loophole
The modern sophisticate's choice. Here, asymmetry is key.

The Whiplash Classic
Also looks great tucked into a suit.

The Jedi
For superior intellects. And people who don't live in Chicago.

....

The *SARTORIAL CANON*

≫ • ≪

The Accessories

....

ALFRED DUNHILL ➤ When Alfred Dunhill inherited his father's London saddlery in 1893, he turned it into an outfitter for pioneering motorists. The firm gradually extended into the wider realm of men's luxury leather goods, watches, accessories, and writing instruments. Since 1924, for instance, Dunhill has been a source of sophisticated lighters, including the Unique, a classic design that can be operated with one hand. www.dunhill.com

HERMÈS ➤ For men, the French luxury-goods company Hermès is much more than its famous silk print ties, a Wall Street status symbol during the 1980s. Hermès was founded in 1837 as a saddler, and its leather accessories remain incomparable—belts, wallets, agendas, and gloves with a masculine heft and a sophisticated color palette. www.hermes.com

PERSOL ➤ In 1957, the 90-plus-year-old Italian eyewear company Persol created its most famous dark glasses, Model 649, for Turin's tram drivers. Marcello Mastroianni wore a pair in the 1961 movie *Divorce Italian Style*, as did Steve McQueen in 1968's *The Thomas Crown Affair*. The brand's trademark silver arrow, flexible stem, and unmistakable Italian lines never go out of style. www.persol.com

ROLEX ➤ The century-old Swiss firm Rolex is—no surprise—the world's biggest luxury watch brand. If imitation is the sincerest form of flattery, the Rolex watch has a lot of admirers. The company makes oversize watches for deep-sea diving, aviation, and mountain climbing. But Rolex can do simple and compact, too, as in the pleasingly modest Air-King. www.rolex.com

VALEXTRA ➤ No logo or identifying lettering—not even a discrete "V"—mars the impeccable surfaces of the suitcases, overnight bags, briefcases, and smaller goods produced by the low-key, 92-year-old Milanese firm. Valextra's traditional satchel briefcase, made in the company's trademark Havana-colored saddle leather, is the ultimate in understated luxury. www.valextra.it

CHAPTER SEVEN

Personal Care

....

YOU CAN WALK INTO A PARTY
wearing a Brioni suit and a $600 pair of shoes,
but if you have a lame haircut, and
your hands and skin look like you just stumbled off
the red-eye, you might as well have shopped at the Gap,
pocketed the extra money, and used it to stoke
your backyard grill. ➤

....

UNLESS YOU REALLY have just gotten off the red-eye, that is—but that only excuses the skin.

GETTING A GOOD haircut is as important as wearing a suit that fits properly, and in fact it's been an important element of personal care for millennia. Personal care might mean merely "a shave and a haircut" to many men, but back in the day—and we mean *way* back, from ancient Assyria to eighteenth-century England—barbers were known as surgeons, and they rendered what passed for professional medical, dental, and hygiene services. The traditional barber's pole, its red and white stripes symbolizing blood and bandages, is the last vestige of the haircutter's former multiple roles. As a rule, a visit to the barber is no longer life threatening, unless you happen to be an Italian mobster (legendary New York *mafioso* Albert Anastasia and his fictional counterpart, Moe Green in *The Godfather,* were both offed in their padded barber chairs). But an inappropriate or inept haircut can rub out the effect of your ass-kicking suit in an equally brutal manner.

WITH A FEW NOTABLE EXCEPTIONS, such as Romantic poets, Aquarian hippies, and dreadlocked Rastafarians, neat, simple, and short—give or take a few inches—has been the haircut of choice for the mainstream male since the disappearance of wigs in the eighteenth century. But short doesn't mean that anyone wielding a sharp pair of scissors can do the job. Find a good barber or stylist, and stick with him or her like white on rice. (We're sorry, but girlfriends and mothers do not qualify.)

THE DISAPPEARANCE OF WIGS saw the introduction of hair products such as Victorian macassar oil, designed to keep hairstyles sleek and in place. In the 1920s, men used pomades—waxy preparations that make the hair look slick and glossy—to achieve the streamlined Art Deco look epitomized by matinee idol Rudolph Valentino. Such industrial-strength styling products had largely fallen out of use by the 1960s, but lighter-touch gels, mousses, and pastes began showing up in the 1980s, along with mohawks, mullets, and other manner of ill-conceived styles for the head. Most "product" today is easier to apply than its gooey predecessors, though you may need more patience than Job to decipher the selection in your local drugstore. The best advice: Ask your stylist for a recommendation, and don't buy the cheapest crap you can find.

HAIR, INEVITABLY, PRESENTS problems. Some men watch themselves go bald, while others struggle to free themselves of superfluous hair that sprouts invasively from sites all over their bodies. Men have been shaving off their facial hair since prehistoric times, and Alexander the Great insisted his troops be clean-shaven so the enemy couldn't grab hold of their beards. This all seemed to unravel after Rome fell and the hirsute Goths descended, and today, frankly, facial hair is entirely a matter of personal choice. The rule here is that mustaches, beards, and sideburns should be neatly trimmed. Leave bushy beards to Grizzly Adams and under-the-chin numbers to the Amish. The second rule of facial hair: No one wants to see your nose or ears looking like party favors. Trim regularly, using extreme care (see p. 177).

AN EXPANDING MENU of cosmetic and grooming treatments—including facials, manicures, pedicures, massages, and body wraps—is offered by another recent phenomenon: full-service men's day spas. Before you start snickering, you might want to know that most of these establishments create a traditionally masculine environment: dark-wood-and-leather gentleman's-club decor is a favorite. Essentially, the new spas are taking the classic barber shop experience and expanding it—not by reinstating the dental and surgical services they offered in the past but by catering to the modern man's healthy desire to look and feel his best.

BATHROOM CABINET

What does your bathroom have in it? Examine our list and check where applicable.

➠ RAZOR

Two blades? Three? Forget the gizmos. Find a handsome razor that's well balanced and is compatible with good blades.

➠ HAIR TEXTURIZER

A mild relaxer that loosens the curl of the hair, separates individual hairs, and makes your hair generally easier to manage.

➠ BODY WASH

It won't slip out of your hands in the shower, smells good, and unlike soap, travels well.

➠ SPF 15 LIP BALM

Lips burn, too. Just like ears. Use an SPF balm to protect from the sun's rays and prevent cracking in winter.

➠ SHAMPOO

Find one that's suitable for your hair type, and use it every second or third day (unless you're training for the Iron Man—then it's *every* day).

➠ ALCOHOL-FREE DEODORANT

Smelling clean is just as important as looking good—but not at the expense of dessicated armpits.

➠ CONDITIONER

No, it's not a waste of time—it works to make your hair softer and less dry in winter. Some even help to control dandruff.

➠ HAND-AND-BODY LOTION

Odysseus used olive oil; you should use something that doesn't make you smell like salad.

➠ SHAVING CREAM

Creams and gels that come in aerosol cans dry your skin. Find one in a tub or jar and that preferably contains lanolin or a hypoallergenic substitute.

➠ AFTERSHAVE BALM

Restores moisture to the skin and relieves mild post-shave irritation. Avoid products with a high alcohol content.

➠ SOAP

All soap washes off dirt and bac-teria—you don't need deodorant and antibacterial soaps. Those made from a base of vegetable glycerin are kinder to your face.

➠ TOENAIL CLIPPERS

If your toenails are scratching her shins, it's time to use them.

➠ SPF 15 MOISTURIZER

The sun is stronger—and you're exposed to it more often—than you think. Use it every day.

➠ BADGER-HAIR SHAVING BRUSH

Gives your face the optimum slippery protection from the razor blade.

Your Hair Has a Life of Its Own.

How to deal with the inevitable: graying, overly styled, and thinning hair

---

Frequently Asked Questions

Q *My graying hair makes me look fifteen years older than I am. What should I do?*
Simple—dye it. Thanks to improved technology, which makes for drastically shorter dyeing time and greater subtlety, a huge number of men are turning to color jobs. You probably even know a couple of guys who do it, and you have no idea because modern dyes camouflage the gray rather than completely cover it, and fade out gradually over time.

Getting it done once every two haircuts should be plenty—it's just a ten-minute rinse at the washbasin. We strongly recommend going to a salon, but if you must do it at home, remember: Most people think their hair is darker than it really is. So when choosing your color, grab one shade lighter. Expect to leave the dye in for a little less than the recommended time if you have fine hair. And although we don't suggest going against the instructions, no matter how long you leave it in, it's difficult to overdye your hair. Unless, of course, you're Wayne Newton.

Q *When I use gel, my hair looks too "styled."*
First off, where did you buy your gel? If it came in a jumbo container from Costco, you may be damaging more than just your image. Cheap gel strips hair and causes dryness. Trash it. You probably shouldn't be using gel at all. If you want a natural look—but nothing too shabby—opt for creams. They're softer on your hair than gels. For more hold,

Official HAIRSTYLES for MEN

IVY LEAGUE
CREW CUT
FLAT TOP WITH FENDERS
THE PREEMPTIVE STRIKE

use pastes or waxes. Apply a little—a good dime-sized drop—then add more as you need to. Your hair should be damp before it takes on a shape. Emulsify in your palm and apply to the roots, working your way out, then use your hands to style, never a brush or a blow-dryer.

Q *I'm losing my hair. And it makes me sad.*
The only dignified way to deal with balding or thinning hair is to learn to live with it. Nay,

learn to love it. Confidence (and a good cut) is more attractive than any treatment. Trying to conceal it will only draw attention, generally of the pointing, laughing, and snickering variety. Never create length to hide thinning hair; the longer it is, the skimpier it looks. You want short-cropped cut, which will make your hair appear thicker. Or you can forget all of the above and do what Bruce Willis was man enough to do: use a disposable razor. Shave every other day, or even every day if you want that nice, intimidating shine. Just don't forget the sunscreen.

If you're too proud, stubborn, or deluded to admit defeat, you have two options: Good (expensive) transplants have come so far that even hair professionals often can't tell the difference. There's also Propecia, a prescription medication that treats moderate male pattern baldness. Results are often noticeable in three months.

{ The RULES }
•
HAIRSTYLES THAT HAVE NAMES should never appear on your head. The mullet, the wedge, and the fauxhawk, for example.

**HAIR APPARENT:
THE DONALD TRUMP**
➤ *You have to hand it to
Donald Trump: the tycoon
has never lacked the courage
of his convictions. His hair-
style is no exception. It's an
assertion of control and an
expression of his approach
to business—every hair is in
place, and nothing is left to
chance. Grooming may take
a little extra time, but for a
businessman whose strategy
depends on being in the public
eye, it's time well spent.*

FIVE TERMS TO USE WITH YOUR BARBER

You know how you want your hair to look, but you don't know how to explain it.
Here are five terms your barber will understand.

THINNED OUT	LAYERED	CHOPPY	RAZORED	TEXTURIZED

• **THINNED OUT**
When the barber breaks out thinning shears (which look like regular scissors but have matching sets of "teeth" with gaps between them), which allow some of the hairs to be cut short and others to remain at their full length. Good for thick, unmanageable hair.

• **LAYERED**
When longer hair rests on top of shorter hair, and your hair appears to have some movement and depth. Good for thin hair.

• **CHOPPY**
When hairs are all different lengths, which gives hair a thicker appearance. Good for fine or thinning hair.

• **RAZORED**
When a barber uses a razor (instead of scissors) to trim the ends of your hair. Your hairs will have a tapered edge (rather than a blunt, straight-cut edge), which will give them more texture and volume.

• **TEXTURIZED**
Like choppy, only shorter.

THE HAIRCUT RULES
Or, how not to look like a jerk at the salon

• **Great haircuts** result from great cutters of hair and from a consistent working relationship with a barber or stylist who knows your taste and needs. Such people are unlikely to be employed by a business whose name is a pun (Mane Event, Curl Up & Dye, et cetera), and they are unlikely to provide their services for ten bucks. • **Never come straight from the gym.** A good gauge of the appeal of your hair is the amount of time the assistant runs water on your head before touching you. The longer it runs, the more you should consider regular bathing. • **If you're offered a robe,** be sure to take off your collared shirt. It makes your stylist's job easier. • **It's fine to read the paper or a book.** But your cell phone or PDA should stay in your pocket. • **While it is perfectly acceptable to** request a particular stylist, it's creepy when you ask for a favorite shampoo girl. • **Tip your stylist at least 10 percent;** 20 percent or more around the holidays will get you special consideration the rest of the year for things like free touch-ups and preferential scheduling. For your hair washer, 5 percent is plenty.

HAIR APPARENT: THE SIR BEN KINGSLEY

➡ *That Ben Kingsley, faced with thinning hair, should shave his head seems unremarkable. But as recently as the 1980s, razor-assisted baldness was a very rare celebrity phenomenon. With few exceptions, men in the public eye fought tooth and toupee against hair loss. Perhaps Michael Jordan's shaved pate changed the game, but soon we were looking at the bare scalps of Bruce Willis, Moby, Sir Ben, and many other boldface names. Not to mention the guy sitting in the next cubicle.*

THE SUGGESTION
Mind the Beard Line

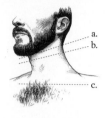

a.
b.
c.

MANY YEARS AGO, growing a beard was easy. You just stopped shaving. Where your beard ended–chin, neck, or somewhere after your chest hair began–was nobody's concern, least of all yours. Now things are different. People tend to have jobs and fewer diseases, and beards require more tailoring. Stay in control of your beard, and you stay in the fight. Stopped too close to the jawbone (line a), a beard makes you look uptight. Left to wander down your neck (line c), however, a beard invites comparisons to feral creatures or iconic communist firebrands. The safest bet is the one-inch band just above your Adam's apple (line b). Here you manage to have both a legitimate beard and something of a neck. You have just as good a grip on machismo and gravitas as you do on an employable future.

How to SHAVE

The average guy will shave about 20,000 times in his lifetime. Get it right, and save the pain.

{ PREPARE }
To get a close, comfortable shave, the hairs of the beard and mustache need to be soft. Heat and moisture get them that way. Ideally, you should shave after a hot shower; failing that, holding a damp, steaming towel against your face for several minutes achieves almost equal results. Warmth also relaxes the skin, reducing the occurrence of nicks and razor burn.

{ LATHER }
Apply a little shaving oil to the face prior to lathering; the blades will slide over it, cutting the hairs without touching the skin. Then lather up. We recommend using shaving cream from a tube for best results. With a badger-hair shaving brush, whip the cream into a rich froth with hot water in a shaving mug, then apply.

{ SHAVE }
With proper preparation and an immaculate blade, two strokes of the razor are enough. First, draw the razor with the grain of the hair; this will remove about 80 percent of the whiskers. Then re-lather and make a return stroke against the grain, cleaning up the remainders. Always use a light touch, letting the blade, not pressure, do the work.

{ PROTECT }
Rinse your face with cold water, then apply a moisturizing lotion. Do not use alcohol-based aftershaves, which dry the skin.

I'M NOT A MASOCHIST, BUT I ALWAYS TAKE A COLD SHOWER IN THE MORNING. IT'S A GREAT BEGINNING OF THE DAY, BECAUSE NOTHING CAN BE WORSE AFTERWARD.

—Roman Polanski

A Simple Guide to Body-Hair Removal

BODY PART	NECESSARY	TOOL	HAZARDS	HOW OFTEN?
NOSE	Yes	Small scissors; electric nose-hair trimmer	With scissors, you could pierce your septum. Otherwise, none.	Check for errant hairs once a week and act accordingly.
EAR	Yes	Shaving razor for lobe; small scissors	Inserting anything into your ear canal could lead to damage. Don't.	As needed
BACK	Only if your back hair makes you uncomfortable. If not, leave it.	Wax (administered by a professional); laser removal	Wax: Bursts of pain followed by horrendous acne breakouts. Laser: Debilitating pain, expensive.	Once a year, six weeks before you'll take your shirt off in public.
CHEST	Only if the hair becomes obtrusive. Or if it's starting to look like Bob Marley's head.	Small scissors or electric hair clipper	Cutting yourself; over-trimming your way back to early puberty.	As soon as the hair becomes visible through a thin polo shirt.
NETHER REGIONS	Only when mandated by a physician or significant other.	Small scissors	Too many to count, too horrible to name.	As rarely as possible.

OUT-OF-CONTROL

Eyebrows

What to do when your eyebrows are growing like kudzu

A LOT OF PEOPLE think eyebrows are something you can take care of at home, but they're too easy to overdo, and you can end up looking worse than when you started. If you refuse to spend a couple bucks getting waxed or plucked by a pro, at least heed their advice. First off, get a good pair of tweezers. Be sure to get slanted tips; pointed tweezers are more likely to rip the hair or pinch your skin. The best time to pluck is right after a warm shower, when the hairs are easier to pull out. As for what to remove, put the pad of your thumb between your brows; whatever hair it covers needs to be gone. Carefully brush your brows up and trim the hairs that stray over your brow line. Whatever you do, don't mess with your lower brow line. Touch that and you risk giving your eyebrows shape. Only women should have shaped eyebrows.

HAIR APPARENT: THE ROBERT DE NIRO
➡ *Grizzled elegance appears to be Robert De Niro's watchword. Unshaven, with tousled hair, De Niro seems to be saying "I can't be bothered," while his haircut says, "Oh yes, I can." The rule here: If you're going for an unkempt look, it always helps to have a great haircut and a good suit, and you'd better make sure you smell nice. Oh, and if you're a movie star, that's a big bonus, too.*

FACIAL-HAIR STRATEGIES

ACCEPTABLE	**RISKY**	**UNACCEPTABLE**

HOW TO USE YOUR FACIAL HAIR

According to pogonologists (beard experts), the right facial hair can accentuate or minimize the features you were born with. Below are four examples of common problems, along with suggestions for using facial hair to fix them.

fig. 1

Your Philtrum is Huge
Solution: A relatively thick mustache will fill in the space (see fig. 1), or go with a long, full beard to even things out and draw attention away from that giant space between your nose and top lip.

Your Face is Skinny
Solution: A short, scruffy beard will add some width, fill in your cheeks, and convince any loitering raptors to move on.

Your Face is Fat
Solution: Grow your beard and square off the bottom to create the illusion of a strong—and single—chin. And let it grow down your neck at least an inch and a half past your last chin.

Your Face is Really Round
Solution: A goatee will elongate your face. Longer sideburns will help accentuate, or make it look like you have, cheekbones.

What a Close Shave Feels Like

Every man should sit down for a professional shave at least once. For $20 to $60, you'll learn what can be achieved with a sharp blade in a steady hand. Until you do, read on. This is what a good shave is about:

After the barber has finished with the shave—after he has draped your face with steamed towels of exquisite cotton; after he has applied a moisturizing gel to your mug; after he has covered you once more with the steamed towel; after he has brushed the powder into a rich foam on your chops and artistically removed your whiskers, first in one direction and then in the other (and it is artistic—a good Italian *barbiere* regards you as a sculptor regards his masterpiece, with eyes narrowed, appraisingly); after he has covered your face yet another time with a towel and briskly applied a tonic of your choosing—after all that, he takes the sheet with which he wrapped your face at the very beginning of the process, folds it exactly once, and then uses it to fan that tonic and your smooth and restored face dry.

How to Seal the Deal

With a good-lookin' handshake

DON'T CUT YOUR CUTICLES, *that thin layer of skin that grows over the base of each nail. It's not sanitary, and it's not safe. Push them back with your fingertips after you shower, when your skin is softest.*

SMOOTH THE EDGES. *Nail files are just as important as they are embarrassing, but having your nails fully rounded will keep you from picking at them. Don't try to use the little file on your clippers—get a real one.*

MOISTURIZE. *We know, we know, it's a little girlie, but applying lotion daily can help prevent cracked and painful skin. If you insist on keeping some at work, keep it in a drawer and apply discreetly.*

LEAVE A LITTLE BIT OF WHITE *at the tips of your nails. Cutting too close to the nail bed can cause infections and frustration when you find a spare penny. It's time to trim when you touch the end of your finger and can feel your nail.*

STOP USING YOUR TEETH. *Don't bite, chew, or gnaw on nails, hangnails, or cuticles. This is what separates us from animals. If you've got a hangnail, cut it away with a pair of sharp scissors.*

NO BUFFING, NOT EVER. *A slight natural shine looks presentable, but more than that and you'll have a hard time convincing someone that you're not wearing polish.*

Skin Care 101: CLEANSE! EXFOLIATE! MOISTURIZE!

cleanse every day. A good antibacterial soap works fine if you have oily skin; a gentle non-soap cleanser is better if your skin is dry. Use warm, not hot, water—you want to open your pores gently, not scald them—and a washcloth, which is a better gunk remover than your bare hands.

exfoliate once a week. It will remove the top layer of dead cells, which make your skin look dull, and get rid of any deep-seated grime

along with them. Use an exfoliating face scrub instead of your regular soap or cleanser. More frequent use will irritate your skin.

moisturize and apply sunscreen every day. Always use a moisturizer with sunscreen, unless your skin is oily, in which case use a mildly astringent toner followed by an oil-free sunscreen. SPF 15 is more than adequate for the work environment, as long as you're not a lifeguard.

The Perfect
*DOPP KIT**

THIS IS THE PERFECT DOPP KIT.
To the untrained eye, it may look like
other, nonperfect Dopp kits, but here's
why it's perfect: It's made of nylon, so
it's washable and suited to the messy
rough-and-tumble of travel. Also, it's a
shallow rectangle that you can stack in
your bag. Finally, it's roomy enough to
hold all of the following, which is more
or less what every man should carry.

Body wash	*Nail clippers*
Deodorant	*Lint roller*
Lip balm	*Extra pair of contact lenses*
Razor	
Shaving cream	*Band-aids*
	Airborne
Shampoo	*Earplugs*
Moisturizer-sunscreen combo	*Floss*
	Condoms
Toothbrush and toothpaste	*Ibuprofen*

*And Other Dopp Kit Essentials

A crisp $20 bill
What's that, you say? You've
lost your wallet and have no
access to cash? It's a good
thing you've got a $20 bill
tucked away in your Dopp
kit. Plus, as you know, the bill
measures six and one-eighth
inches long, so you can use it
to measure things—that is, if
you haven't already given it to
the bellhop.

A book of matches
You never know when, and
where, you'll need to light a
woman's cigarette. They also
come in handy when enjoying
a flaming shot of Bacardi out of
your hotel's minibar.

A safety pin
Use it to fasten a shirt if a
button has popped, to pick an
old-fashioned lock, to fix small
tears, to fasten your pants if the
zipper breaks, or to replace a
lost screw in your sunglasses.
The uses are myriad, but
remember to fasten it so that
the bulkier ends don't show.

The **SARTORIAL CANON**

≫ • ≪

Personal Care

DOVO SOLINGEN	➤ For more than a century, Dovo, a small, family-owned steelworks, has been producing high-quality razors, scissors, and clippers in Solingen, a German town synonymous with the knife and cutlery industry. Their Merkur single-blade safety razors are practical, beautiful instruments; their manicure kits are meticulously designed. www.dovo.com
KIEHL'S	➤ Kiehl's opened as an old-world apothecary in New York's East Village back in 1851. It has been in the same location ever since, selling a range of unique skin and hair products in pleasingly generic plastic bottles and tubes with no-nonsense, informative labels. Kiehl's low-key men's products are all recommendable, though Facial Fuel SPF 15 is a cream no male epidermis should do without. www.kiehls.com
PENHALIGON'S	➤ Barber William Penhaligon set up shop in 1860 next to the Turkish Baths in London's Piccadilly. A decade later, he concocted his first gentlemen's scent, Hammam Bouquet, inspired by the steam and sculpture of the baths. The firm has created scents for the British nobility and produces distinguished masculine fragrances. www.penhaligons.co.uk
R. A. ROONEY	➤ There are several reasons why R. A. Rooney & Sons, London, make the best badger-hair shaving brushes—but mostly because they've done it since the late seventeenth century. Rooney offers several grades of hair: Go for the finest, which is ruinously expensive but will give a lifetime's pleasure. www.executive-shaving.co.uk/rooney-london-brushworks-company.php
TRUEFITT & HILL	➤ Established in 1805, Truefitt & Hill, on St. James's Street, London, has served as the royal barber since the reign of George III. These days the firm has salons in Chicago, Toronto, and Las Vegas, but if you can't make it in for one of their fabled 30-minute straight-razor shaves, you can purchase their luxurious shaving creams and other fine toiletries online. www.truefittandhill.com

●

CHAPTER EIGHT

Your

Wardrobe

....

SUPPOSE YOU'RE A MAN

with a proper day job and a reasonably active after-office-hours life. How many clothes do you need? Fewer than you think. A concise wardrobe that extends seamlessly from dressy to casual, in which each piece coordinates successfully with most of the others, ➡

....

will serve you better over the long run than an enormous collection of trendy, mismatched one-offs—even those with big-name designer labels. From a small but carefully chosen wardrobe, it's possible to conjure an astonishing variety of different looks. But like any conjuring trick, it takes preparation and practice to bring it off convincingly—you're mastering an art, not practicing alchemy.

ONLY YOU CAN DECIDE what specific mix of items belongs in your wardrobe, but you should begin with a core of indispensable pieces, a near-universal sartorial foundation (see pp. 188–91). A navy blue suit, gray flannel trousers, a white cotton dress shirt, a fine wool V-neck sweater, black oxford lace-ups, a handful of well-chosen neckties: These are your building blocks. Absolute basics may sound about as interesting as braised tofu for dinner, but *basic* is not the same thing as *anonymous*, and there are a number of general rules about how to choose wardrobe fundamentals so that you'll never appear to be wearing a bland conformist uniform.

FIRST, UNLESS YOU have a surfeit of money, time, and steely confidence, ignore the latest trends. Good evolutionary design finds its way into the menswear mainstream quickly enough; you don't have to volunteer as a guinea pig in the fashion laboratory. Take your three watchwords—classic, simple, and understated—and think of their mirror images: timeless, long-lasting, recession-proof.

WHATEVER THE ITEM, it should be made of fine-quality fabrics and materials—smooth worsted, lustrous cashmere, supple leather, hefty denim. Two, it should be carefully constructed, using painstaking manufacturing techniques that don't cut necessary corners or skimp on telling details. Three, it should fit you as perfectly as possible. If we've told you once, we've told you a thousand times: No matter how expensive the fabric or finicky the craftsmanship, an ill-fitting garment will look cheap. And four, it should be clean, in good repair, and stored appropriately. Finally, beware the inexpensive designer knock off. Many of these budget reproductions look great—for about five minutes, after which they start to bag, or stretch, or fall apart. Quality is the true economy in style: You get exactly what you pay for, which should always be the best threads you can afford.

OF COURSE, THERE is such a thing as too much good taste, which is why you shouldn't be afraid to add the occasional flourish—maybe even an off-note or two—to your eminently sensible wardrobe. The Italians call it *sprezzatura*. And if, on a visit to France in 1930, the future Duke of Windsor could wear a checked suit with a pink shirt, red-and-white socks, and black-and-tan shoes, it doesn't seem such a sartorial risk today for a man to sport burnt-orange socks, for example, and brown suede oxfords with his gray flannel suit.

HERE'S WHERE WE move beyond the careful selection of the basics to the more elusive art of putting them together. There's a lesson to be learned from Fred Astaire, perhaps the most sophisticated dresser this country has ever produced: The man who made dressing elegantly—and dancing perfectly— look absolutely effortless worked very hard at both. When, in 1923, the future Duke of Windsor went backstage to congratulate Astaire on his first London stage appearance, the dancer wrote: "All the time I was taking special notice of how he was dressed—impeccably in tails. HRH was unquestionably the best-dressed young man in the world, and I was missing none of it." The next morning, Astaire went to Savile Row and ordered a waistcoat exactly like the duke's. More recently—and less generously—Mick Jagger joked about David Bowie, "Never wear a new pair of shoes in front of him." The point is, all of us should feel free to be inspired by—hell, to steal from—our best-dressed contemporaries. You're not born with a flawless sartorial sense; you develop it. Studying the masters of personal style is a great way to begin training your own taste.

WARDROBE

The ten things you'll need in your closet. You take care of the socks and underwear.
Follow our advice about the rest.

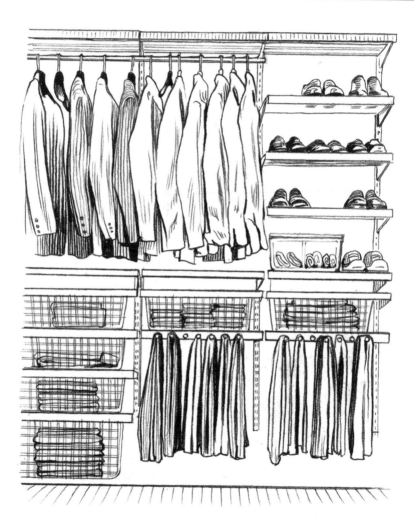

➥ WHITE OXFORD BUTTON-DOWN SHIRT

The white button-down can be worn with a suit and tie, on its own with a pair of jeans, or underneath a sweater.

➥ LIGHTWEIGHT CASHMERE V-NECK SWEATER

A thin cashmere sweater can be worn every month save for August. Goes with jeans or underneath a suit jacket.

➥ SUNGLASSES

Obvious for their functionality (that whole sun-in-the-eyes thing), but also necessary as an accessory that adds the all-important final touch.

➥ A DARK PAIR OF JEANS

Make sure they are crisp and able to be worn with a T-shirt, button-down, or the jacket from your suit.

➥ ONE SET OF CEDAR SHOE TREES

You need only one pair, to keep your just-worn shoes in good shape.

➥ WHITE, GRAY, AND BLACK T-SHIRTS

Sleep in them, wear them to the gym, or use them underneath a shirt or sweater.

➥ BLACK LACE-UPS

Clean, dressy black lace-up shoes will work with any color suit and still look at home at the foot of your jeans.

➥ OVERNIGHT BAG

Because a man never knows when he might have to flee at a moment's notice, make sure it's big enough to carry two nights' worth of stuff.

➥ THREE-BUTTON NAVY SUIT

Navy is the most versatile color for a man's suit. Extend its life by wearing it with a shirt and tie, or wear just the jacket with jeans and a button-down.

➥ MEDIUM-WIDTH TIE

If it's too skinny or too fat, you limit the types of shirts you can wear with it. A medium width, in a neutral color and pattern, has the most versatility.

CARY GRANT

➤ *As with a few other great romantic stars, a wardrobe of superbly tailored clothes was an essential part of Cary Grant's mystique. The impeccable suits seemed like a second skin, as integral to his legendary presence as the cleft in his chin. Grant, the star of thrillers like* To Catch a Thief *and* Notorious, *personified the ageless Hollywood male lead of the 1940s and 1950s, and the era's standard of sophistication and charm. That blend of sartorial and personal perfection was the fantasy self-image of many men. Even Cary Grant said he wanted to be Cary Grant.*

Build a Working Wardrobe:

The 5 Shirts, 4 Ties, 3 Suits, 2 Shoes, and 1 Overcoat You Need

These are the building blocks of a solid working wardrobe. Once you've got them covered, you can experiment with more color and pattern. But start out with these essentials and you'll always be ready for the office.

5 SHIRTS
The shirt should have a supporting role in one's outfit. It's a backdrop–utility is paramount. Keep the color simple and it will go with everything.

- 1 plain white French-cuff
- 1 plain blue French-cuff
- 1 dark-and-light-blue Benegal-stripe French-cuff
- 1 blue button-down oxford button-cuff
- 1 white button-down oxford button-cuff

4 TIES
Simple always looks sharpest.

- 1 plain navy (killer on a white shirt)
- 1 regimental stripe (bold but refined)
- 1 subdued paisley or pattern (for variety)

3 SUITS
Because you should never wear the same suit two days in a row.

- 1 navy two- or three-button wool suit. Your most flexible investment, good for postwork and fine for the boardroom, too.
- 1 charcoal flannel suit, single-breasted, two-or three-button
- 1 mid-gray glenurquhart or pinstripe, in lightweight wool

2 PAIRS OF SHOES
Because shoes need a day off just like suits.

- 1 pair of plain black cap-toe oxford lace-ups, in calfskin. To get you through the day and well into the night.
- 1 pair of chestnut-brown, fine-cut wing-tips. They go with everything except a black suit—which you don't need, anyway.

1 OVERCOAT
Well chosen, it's an investment that will last for years.

- 1 navy or black wool or cashmere fly-front overcoat, knee length and close fitting.

LIKE A MILLION BUCKS

The $1,000 Wardrobe

The $2,000 Wardrobe

THE STRATEGY

If it's leather, don't go cheap. Pay a little extra for your shoes and your belt. (You do wear them the most, after all.) Beyond that, simple essentials such as a navy blue or a gray suit and both a white and a dark dress shirt will serve you well in any scenario.	If you've got two grand to spend, chances are you're the type of guy who finds himself in more-formal situations. Make sure to nab yourself a luxurious tie, and don't skimp on the shoes. With the extra cash, you can now extend into the casual as well, with some dark jeans and a duffel bag to tote it all around in.

STARTING FROM SCRATCH

A good navy blue suit and a pair of quality black oxford lace-ups. If you have cash left over, spend at least $100 on a white cotton dress shirt.	See left. Add to this a pair of brown leather wing-tips, dress shirts in varied cuff and collar styles, and a couple of nice accessories, like a thick silk tie and a leather weekend bag.

IF YOU'RE UPGRADING

Add an alternate suit (gray, for example) and a shoe—brown wing-tips look good with nearly everything. As above, throw in a nice dress shirt with French cuffs.	A black cashmere sweater and a first-rate topcoat—or, if you're a permanent resident of L.A. or Miami, substitute a good summer-weight suit and fine linen or cotton sweater.

FOUR STRATEGIES, FOUR PRICE RANGES: STEP-BY-STEP INSTRUCTIONS FOR BUILDING A PREMIUM WARDROBE THAT WORKS WITH YOUR BUDGET

The $4,000 Wardrobe	*The $5,000 Wardrobe*

THE STRATEGY

Here is where you begin reaching the upper echelons of fine tailoring. So spend on quality in your suit and jacket. Add versatile cashmere to your casual stuff, and spend a little extra on some fine cotton in your shirts. A leather duffel will last you a lifetime.	You're living the dream. And so you're going to need a few nice shirts, one for lunch at the Four Seasons and another for dinner at Morton's. You'll change your tie, too. So get two of those and a pocket square to go with them. You're spending four figures on your suit and jacket, so make sure they're tailored just right.

STARTING FROM SCRATCH

Make sure you have a fine pair of leather shoes. Then go for a top-quality or made-to-measure suit, a couple of custom-made shirts, and a superior accessory, like a lizard wallet.	You either won the lottery or at blackjack in Vegas. If you don't have a suit, splurge on bespoke. And for God's sake, get yourself a pair of handcrafted leather shoes.

IF YOU'RE UPGRADING

Impeccably tailored sport jackets, one in cashmere and one in tweed, and a couple more cashmere sweaters. Smart, strong luggage is essential if you travel frequently.	Go for broke on premium shirts and accessories—a beautifully detailed leather briefcase, for example. Or easily spend your $5K on a good-looking luxury watch.

Unless He's Headed to a Black-tie Wedding,
A MAN ALWAYS HAS OPTIONS

	DAYTIME BARBECUE	SUMMER COCKTAIL PARTY	DRINKING IN A BAR	HOLIDAY PARTY
GOOD	*Khaki chinos, polo shirt, brown loafers*	*Cotton chinos, crisp oxford button-down, blue wool blazer*	*Light-blue jeans, button-down shirt*	*Corduroy pants, crewneck sweater*
BETTER	*Red or blue chinos, short sleeved rugby shirt, white canvas sneakers*	*Linen trousers, rumpled oxford button-down, seersucker blazer*	*Dark-blue jeans, long-sleeved rugby shirt*	*Flannel trousers, turtleneck, cardigan sweater*
NEVER	*Cargo shorts, tank top, flip-flops, lifeguard whistle*	*Jeans or shorts, bright madras blazer*	*Sweatpants, sport jersey*	*Anything depicting Rudolf, Santa, or the Baby Jesus*

{ *The RULES* }

•

THINGS THE AMERICAN MAN CAN'T WEAR TO A FUNERAL: *A bow tie, whimsical patterns, a light colored coat, a silk pocket square, denim (unless the ceremony involves pouring out cans of Schlitz). At your own funeral? Wear whatever you please.*

•

OFFICIALLY STATED DRESS CODES YOU CAN ALWAYS BEND: *Black-tie, business casual, casual.*

•

OFFICIAL DRESS CODES YOU CAN'T: *Cocktail formal, white-tie, morning dress.*

HOW TO
Dress for an Occasion

It's the hosts' rules that matter. If they have made no specific remarks on the invitation, go with convention. And then dress even better.

Anything that involves births, bar mitzvahs, marriages, or deaths requires your respect— even if you're not a believer in any of it. Religious ceremonies generally require a jacket.

•

For Islamic ceremonies, shoes are removed during prayer. Make sure you're wearing fresh, unholed socks.

•

Read the invite. If a wedding is in an unusual location, dress accordingly. Formal wear on a beach doesn't work (unless you're the groom). But if the setting is an official place of worship, wear a sober suit. A charcoal or dark navy suit will cover you for all eventualities.

THE DUKE OF WINDSOR
➤ *Probably no clotheshorse had more influence on twentieth-century men's style than the Duke of Windsor. His sophisticated, inventive, and occasionally dotty personal wardrobe was featured constantly in magazines, newspapers, newsreels, and, later, on television—and men everywhere wanted to dress as he did. The ensemble depicted here includes several of his sartorial innovations: the hefty Windsor tie knot; a V-neck sweater worn as a vest; boldly graphic tweeds; brown shoes with gray trousers; and above all, a sense that style never compromises comfort.*

A Concise Guide to Patterns

Remember when your grandfather used to wear plaid on plaid? Don't do that.

BY THE BOOK	ALTERNATIVE

KEEP IT SIMPLE by pairing a minor color from your tie with a major color from your shirt. Here, the small dots of blue pick up the blue of the shirt. Similarly, you could match a major color on a tie with a minor shirt stripe.

CONTRARY TO mainstream thinking, you can match a bold geometric tie with a striped shirt without inducing nausea. Don't be afraid to go very bold, in both color and the scale of the pattern.

FOR WATCHES, concentrate on pairing color and material with your cuff links. Here it works because the shapes and colors complement each other perfectly. It would work equally well with a round steel cuff link.

PICK A MINOR color from the pattern of your jacket and pair it with a watch whose color matches it—loosely. Then use the cuff link to create contrast. Avoid steel in favor of colored glass or silk knots. Don't try to match everything.

THE UTTERLY correct sock is one that is barely noticeable beneath the hem of your pants. (The pant legs here have been raised to show the socks.) The color should match your trousers to visually lengthen your legs.

USE YOUR ANKLES as a place to add some color. Note that this works only if you maintain strict sobriety everywhere else in the outfit: plain black or very dark brown shoes and little or no pattern anywhere else.

SOME COLORS ARE
MEANT TO BE TOGETHER. SOME ARE NOT.

Below, the combinations that do and do not work.

YES

JACKETS	BROWN	GRAY	BLACK	NAVY	NAVY
PANTS	NAVY	NAVY	GRAY	GRAY	BROWN
SHOES	BLACK	BROWN	BLACK	BLACK	BROWN

NO

JACKETS	BROWN	GRAY	BLACK	BLACK	NAVY
PANTS	BLACK	BLACK	NAVY	BROWN	BLACK
SHOES	BROWN	BROWN	BLACK	BLACK	BROWN

The Details That Set You Apart

Watch   Think of it as a clear banner proclaiming your good taste, style, and success. It should not have cost you $24.99.

Cuffs   Should show a quarter inch to a half inch past the jacket sleeve.

Tie   Should always be perfectly knotted, with a single notch or dimple and with the point sitting at the waistband.

Shoes   Elongated, slightly pointed classic Italian, British, or American shoes.

MATCH THESE:
- *Watch, cuff links, belt buckle*
- *Watch strap, shoes, belt*
- *Pocket square with one minor color in your tie or shirt*

NEVER MATCH THESE:
- *Shirt and tie*
- *Tie and pocket square*
- *Socks and shoes*
- *Trousers and shoes (except with a tux)*
- *Shirt and suit*

How to Pull Off a
SUMMER LOOK

Seersucker	**Madras**	**Linen**	**Summer wool**
It comes in all kinds of snazzy colors and patterns these days. Ignore them and stick with the classic seersucker stripe—pale blue and off-white—which is classic for a reason. When worn with a white cotton oxford, it's as dressed up as summer weekends should get.	A pair of shorts is as much madras as most eyes can handle. Keep the rest of the outfit simple—e.g., a navy blue blazer and a white shirt—and under no circumstances should it include another madras garment. A muted madras blazer worn with a great pair of jeans is another possibility.	Like convertibles and ball-park hot dogs, a deconstructed linen suit is a summer privilege and should not be abused. All the rules of tailoring still apply, and while a slight wrinkle may convey casual cool, a crumpled, just-rolled-out-of-bed look does not.	Unless your name is Thurston Howell III or George W. Bush, summer is not one long string of casual parties. When formality calls, a lightweight wool suit can pull heat away from your skin and help keep you cool. To brighten things up, pair it with a light-colored shirt and tie.

How to Pull Off a
WINTER LOOK

Polyester	**Waxed cotton**	**Fur trim**	**Cashmere**
We're going to guess your workplace is heated—and that you're not a high school wrestler trying to cut weight. Lay off the layers during the workweek to minimize sweating. A lightweight polyester jacket in black or dark gray looks good with both suits and casual pairings like jeans and sport jackets.	You may not know a grouse from a partridge, but British hunting attire is damn fine inspiration for casual occasions. A waxed-cotton jacket over twill or moleskin trousers works for urban or country pursuits. Just make sure accessories are polished: dressy boots and leather gloves, for instance.	The fleece-and-jeans combo is warm and easy, but it can feel like a weekend cliché. Add some variety to casual outdoor wear with a nordic-patterned wool sweater over jeans, topped with a smart fur-trimmed anorak. Start with a thin layer of silk, polyester, or polypropylene as a base for warmth.	We've seen it and cringed: a sad old coat or parka defacing a great suit. Whether you're attending a board meeting or the opera, single-digit temperatures are no excuse for sloppiness. An immaculate overcoat—here in cashmere—is a symbol of the professional and the gentleman.

THE UPPER CLASS

THE UPPER CLASS
How to Travel in Superior Style

- Dress comfortably for air travel, but dress up. Exhibit A: Marlon Brando, above, arriving at Orly in 1959.
- Never fly on business-class-only flights. The whole point of flying business class is to have someone you can pity ten rows back.
- If, however, you're flying coach, dress for first class. Track pants, carpet slippers, and a ratty old T-shirt won't get you an upgrade.
- Ensure your carry-on luggage is of sufficient quality and is well cared for—it gets scoped by your fellow passengers.
- Wear big, dark sunglasses at all times. Even on night flights.
- Carry both yours and hers. Real men don't roll.
- And smile... Jet lag is for wimps.

What to pack for the
CASUAL VACATION*

*Based on two nights and three days; does not include socks, underwear, vaccines, or other small but vital travel items

....

MOUNTAINS
For day: One anorak, two light sweaters, two T-shirts, one turtleneck, one pair of jeans, one pair of hiking boots, one pair of gloves.
For night: One dress shirt, one pair of dark corduroy pants, one wool blazer.
Don't even think about bringing: Bulky sweaters that overcrowd your suitcase.

....

BEACH
For day: Four T-shirts, two polo shirts, one pair of khaki shorts, one pair of swimming trunks, one pair of flip-flops.
For night: One pair of khaki pants, a crumpled-cotton unlined blazer, two dress shirts, one pair of loafers.
Don't even think about bringing: Your grape-smugglers, pineapple-print Hawaiian shirt.

....

PARIS
For day: One pair of jeans, one sweater, two T-shirts, one pair of comfortable walking shoes.
For night: One pair of trousers, two dress shirts, one pair of loafers, a navy blue lightweight wool blazer.
Don't even think about bringing: Black beret, "W. Stands for Winner" T-shirt.

....

THE MOON
For day: One space suit, one pair of moon boots, one pair of NASA sweatpants.
For night: One pair of long underwear, an Omega Speedmaster chronograph, a good book, a cyanide pill.
Don't even think about bringing: DVDs of *Apollo 13, 2001: A Space Odyssey,* or *Alien.*

THE DEFINITIVE STYLE RULES

LAYERING

1. Unless you live in Palm Springs, fall and winter weather is rarely predictable. So take a cue from mountaineers: Three thin layers are better than one thick one.

2. The closer to your skin, the thinner the material.

3. A layer can be defined as any piece of clothing that can be worn with dignity on its own.

4. Your spring-break T-shirt from sophomore year does not constitute a layer.

5. A layered combo should always include one piece of luxury, and for luxury, a tailored jacket will always do the trick.

6. Having said that, don't be afraid to shed that luxurious layer when the temperature begins to rise. Nobody likes the sweaty guy, no matter how cool his jacket is.

7. Just because Mother Nature is fond of dreary browns when the weather turns cold, that doesn't mean you have to be. Inject some color by way of a red scarf or a blue sweater. Be fearless.

8. Casual doesn't have to mean jeans. Add some texture and personality below the belt with cords, khakis, or a pair of pinstripe trousers.

9. If you can't put your arms all the way down at your sides, then your sweater's way too thick.

10. Layer just right and you can leave the coat at home.

The ACTIVE MAN'S GUIDE to HOSTILE WEATHER

1. Sunglasses aren't just for summer. The winter sun hangs low in the sky, which means glare. You can't duck to avoid what you can't see.

2. Wear wind briefs. Yes, they look like they were designed for Captain Kirk, but the nylon panel in front does an ace job of protecting the one thing that doesn't get harder in the cold.

3. Unless you want to look like a Campbell's Soup kid, smear some lip balm across your cheeks.

4. Frozen concrete is murder on the feet. When running outdoors, wear a good pair of shoes. If you have no choice but to head indoors, angle the treadmill up at least two degrees to account for the wind resistance it's cheating you out of.

THE EVOLUTION of HIGH-TECH GEAR

Caveman,
1 million years B.C.

Arctic explorer,
1920s

Olympic skier,
1950s

Pro snowboarder,
2008

DENIM is the CENTER of the

CASUAL UNIVERSE

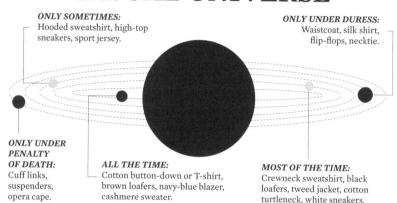

ONLY SOMETIMES:
Hooded sweatshirt, high-top
sneakers, sport jersey.

ONLY UNDER DURESS:
Waistcoat, silk shirt,
flip-flops, necktie.

**ONLY UNDER
PENALTY
OF DEATH:**
Cuff links,
suspenders,
opera cape.

ALL THE TIME:
Cotton button-down or T-shirt,
brown loafers, navy-blue blazer,
cashmere sweater.

MOST OF THE TIME:
Crewneck sweatshirt, black
loafers, tweed jacket, cotton
turtleneck, white sneakers.

TENNIS AND BASEBALL ARE THE

Most Influential Sports on American Style.

DISCUSS.

TENNIS	BASEBALL	BASKETBALL	FOOTBALL	SAILING	BOXING
Lacoste, polo shirts, Rod Laver and Stan Smith sneakers, tennis sweaters	*Brimmed caps, three-quarter-length shirt sleeves, flip-up sunglasses*	*High-top sneakers, mesh shorts*	*XXXL everything*	*Deck shoes, Rolex Yacht-Master*	*Boxer shorts*

{ The RULES }
•
THERE IS A NAME FOR MEN WHO CAN PULL OFF WEARING SPORT JERSEYS.
They're called professional athletes.

JAY-Z

➤ Super-entrepreneur Jay-Z is the new Chairman of the Board—and he dresses for the position. True to his hip-hop roots, the rapper and record executive samples from both sides of the sartorial tracks, faultlessly blending Savile Row swank with sly street funk. That can mean teaming a French-cuffed banker's shirt and silk tie with a full-cut cashmere sweater and baggy jeans. But whatever the particulars, Jay-Z offers a fashion blueprint for the platinum lifestyle.

The Ultimate Closet

How a man should organize his wardrobe

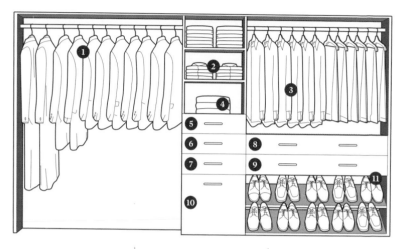

1. SUITS and OVERCOATS
Hang three inches apart to minimize crushing.

2. EXTRA SHIRTS
If you're not planning on wearing them soon, fold and store on a shelf.

3. PRIMARY SHIRTS and TROUSERS
Hang two inches apart to reduce creases.

4. SWEATERS
Fold in piles, and in the off-seasons, store in sealed containers.

5, 6 and 7. SOCKS, UNDERWEAR, T-SHIRTS
Fold neatly.

8. TIES
Fold in half and then roll them up and place along with pocket squares and other accessories.

9. ATHLETIC CLOTHING
All in one place.

10. THICK KNITS and SWEATSHIRTS
Store in deep drawers.

11. SHOES
Keep them on shoe trees and place on sloping shelves.

NOTE:
If your closet doesn't look like this, call an organizing powerhouse immediately.

THE CLOSET RULES

•

Don't overcrowd—stow seasonal items in a separate closet or storage space.

———

Your suit came in a bag for a reason—and not just to transport it home. A storage bag will protect it from insects, fading, and dust.

———

Keep shoes in their shoe bags and boxes to protect them from light and dust.

———

Fold knitwear such as sweaters on a shelf instead of hanging them, to prevent stretching out the shape.

———

Remove dry-cleaned items from wire hangers as soon as you get them home, and hang them on proper hangers.

Know Your Enemy: MOTHS

THE CASEMAKING CLOTHES MOTH (*Tinea pellionella*) and the common webbing clothes moth (*Tineola bisselliella*) are probably already living in your home, hungrily eyeing your wool suits and sweaters. Instinct suggests that killing them will take care of the problem. But it's the moth larvae, not the adults, that do the actual damage. They feed on keratin, a natural protein found in wool, cashmere, mohair, silk, and leather. They're also virtually invisible—so even if you see no adult moths in your closet, that doesn't mean you don't have a problem. How best to solve it?

Laundering and dry cleaning both destroy moth eggs and larvae. Emptying and airing the contents of your wardrobe regularly is also advisable. And vacuuming prime moth hideouts—along baseboards, in closets, under furniture, and along carpet edges—will help rid your home of adults. Dry-clean or wash all wool items before you put them away. For long-term storage—sweaters in summer, lightweight suits in winter—Space Bags or other tight-sealing containers are ideal. Mothballs are just regrettable.

A Field Guide To

Hangers

General purpose, dependable support.

For sport coats only.

For trousers only, by the hem.

For suits.

For breaking into your car.

THE TOOLS

EVERY MAN NEEDS IN HIS WARDROBE

The SHOE-CLEANING KIT
A buffing cloth, some polish, and a couple of brushes. See p. 120 for polishing instructions.

LINT REMOVER
The quick self-adhesive solution to visible fluff, pet hair, and dandruff.

DRAWERS or SHELVES for KNITWEAR
Because they'll last much longer folded flat and laid on a shelf than stuck on a hanger.

The CLOTHES BRUSH
A friend to your suits. Removes stuff you didn't even know was there.

The SHOEHORN
Your shoes will be much better off in the long run.

SHOE TREES
Maintain the shape of your shoes. Will triple their life span.

The BELT-HOLE PUNCH
You need it only once before it's paid for itself.

STITCH WITCHERY
A white-tape wonder that you iron under your trouser hems for short-term take-up solutions.

HANGERS
The right shape for the right garment (see p. 205).

SPACE BAGS
Something you can use to seal against the elements and bugs (see p. 205).

SUIT BAGS
For hanging your more expensive clothing when it's not being worn. Obsessive? No, sensible.

A SLEEVE BOARD
A mini ironing board to get those shirtsleeves looking immaculate.

A GOOD STEAM IRON
Invest in lots of temperature settings, a steam release, and water-spray buttons.

An IRONING BOARD
Because you need something to use the steam iron on.

The SEAM RIPPER
Use this ingenious tool to remove troublesome labels and unpick pocket-basting thread.

COLLAR STAYS
Save the spare collar stiffeners you get when you buy a shirt in a small box. Collar stays get bent out of shape in the wash and often need replacing.

The CLOTHES SHAVER
Used sparingly, an effective way to remove pilling from expensive sweaters.

The PROFESSIONAL STEAMER
The best investment you can make. Save yourself a fortune in dry-cleaning bills (see p. 208).

METAL POLISH
Dip your favorite cuff links in this cleansing solution.

A SMALL BOX in a DRAWER for BITS and PIECES
Stores cuff links, studs, and watches safely in one place.

The Rules of Packing

FOR SMALL SUITCASES

Store your miscellaneous gadgets in an old Dopp kit. It will protect them as well as keep them all in one place.

Save space and save your tie's integrity by rolling it up and placing it safely inside one of your shoes.

Sweaters, especially cashmere, should be folded and laid to the width of the suitcase to prevent bunching and wrinkling.

FOR MEDIUM-SIZE BAGS

Place your lightest pair of shoes at the bottom of your bag. Wear your heaviest; it'll leave your bag lighter.

Your Dopp kit should be slim and shallow and contain travel-sized toothpaste.

Roll small items such as underwear and T-shirts tightly, then use them to hold everything else in your bag in place.

FOR LARGE SUITCASES

Turn your suit jacket inside out. The inner lining, now on the outside, will protect it from wrinkling.

Fold the jacket in on itself along the center of its back, then once more, until you've folded it into quarters.

Wrap the suit in dry-cleaning plastic at the bottom of the suitcase, so it will not move around and crease.

How many times can I wear it

BETWEEN WASHES?

ITEM	ACCEPTABLE WEARINGS	BUT...
Jeans	5 to 10	Fewer if they get visibly dirty or baggy at the knee.
Sweater	10 to 15	Chunkier knits can survive many more.
Sweatshirt	2	Weekends don't count.
T-shirt	1	But two if it's an old favorite.
Dress shirt	1	But two (nonconsecutively) in a real pinch.
Underwear	1	But nothing.
Socks	1	See underwear, above.
Suit	Infinite	Only if you brush, steam, and air regularly.
Coat	Infinite	Only if you brush, steam, and air regularly.

The Endorsement:

The Clothes Steamer

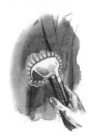

There's a simple tool that can slash your cleaning bills, lengthen your suit's life by several years, and ensure that you always step out the door looking immaculate. It's called a steamer, and you need one. Most natural fibers in suit cloths are susceptible to creasing and bagging in areas of movement (elbow, crotch, knees). Steam works on them as a sauna does on humans, allowing them to relax and regain their natural shape. Unlike harsh cleaning and hot pressing, steam has no ill effects. Spend $80 on a steamer today and it'll pay for itself in six months from the savings on your cleaning bill alone. The technique is simple. Arrange the jacket or trousers on a hanger (ideally one that allows you to work the entire length of the leg in a single stroke). Switch on the steamer and wait until a steady emission of steam develops. Then move the head of the steamer over the cloth in an up-and-down motion, keeping it about two inches from the fabric at all times. The creases will drop out in a matter of seconds, leaving your suit looking as good as new.

Dry Cleaning: *The Truth*

BETWEEN THE SOLVENTS, mechanical agitation, and high drying temperatures, a good suit in the wrong hands can quickly become a thrift-store donation. To protect your investment, choose your dry cleaner wisely. Ask a trusted tailor or retailer for a recommendation.

Clean your suits as infrequently as possible and you'll lengthen their life. Unstained suits can be cleaned once per season, and lightly pressed or steamed in between wearings. But use good judgment: Everyday buildup from dirt, sweat, and cologne can discolor and deteriorate garments, and pressing these contaminants into an item will make the grime permanent.

{ The RULES }

ALMOST ALWAYS BLOT RATHER THAN RUB.
Rubbing damages the fibers, removes dyes, and can spread or set the stain.

ACT QUICKLY. THE LESS TIME THE STAIN SITS,
The better your odds of saving your shirt. Know your limits. You might do more harm than good with oil-based stains. Find a dry cleaner.

If You Witness These Signs,
IT'S TIME TO FIND A NEW CLEANER:

Puckering or bubbling: Threads in garments cleaned at the wrong temperature can shrink, warping the fit.

Shininess Hard pressing can crush fabric fibers and cause a glossy appearance.

Indentations Improper pressing may also leave imprints around pockets and buttons.

To Lengthen
TIME BETWEEN CLEANINGS

• Use a steamer (see opposite page).
• Air out jackets and pants for a few hours before returning them to your closet, so you don't trap moisture.
• The old trick of hanging your suit near the shower for a light steam will save you trips to the cleaners.

Another Reason to Rotate
YOUR WARDROBE

• Giving the suit a few days to hang and relax will help restore its shape.

Esquire's Olde-Fashioned

GUIDE TO DIY STAIN REMOVAL™

PRODUCT	FOR	HOW
Gold Bond Powder	Grease	Sprinkle on stain, let dry, brush off, and wash.
Lemon	Rust	Squeeze onto stain, add salt, and launder.
Hydrogen peroxide	Blood	Apply directly to stain and launder.
Salt	Red wine	Sprinkle on wet stain, let dry, and brush off.
Liquid dishwasher detergent	Anything	Pour on stain and let sit for ten minutes. Wash.
Club soda	Anything	Sponge onto wet stain and dry with towel.
Aspirin	Sweat stains	Drop two pills in water, soak stain in solution.
Rubbing alcohol	Grass	Sponge on and wash.
Cornstarch	Grease	Apply to stain. Let dry.
Hair spray	Ink	Spray onto stain, let dry, and then wash.
Dish soap	Anything	Rub onto stain and rinse.
Shortening	Tree sap	Mix fifty-fifty with water.
White vinegar	Salt	On light fabrics, sponge onto stain and wash.
Nail-polish remover	Nail polish	Apply to stain, let sit, rinse.
Glycerin	Mustard	Apply to stain, let sit, rinse.
OxiClean stain remover	Anything	Follow package directions.
Shampoo	Soiled shirt collar	Brush on and launder.
Clorox Bleach Pen	Anything	Follow package directions.
Borax	Anything	Follow package directions.
Cream of tartar	Chili sauce	Mix with lemon juice, apply, and launder.
Baking soda	Coffee	Add water to make a paste. Apply, let dry, then rinse.

The Esquire Guide to
Longevity

The responsibilities start the moment you take a new piece of clothing home. It's now up to you how long it's going to last.

1. JEANS
Wash your jeans inside out to preserve the indigo dye on the surface and the structure of cotton fibers. **ADD 2 YEARS.**

2. SWEATERS
Wash wool and cashmere by hand using only knitwear-specific detergents like Woolite. Dry flat, spreading the sweater out. **ADD 2 YEARS.**

3. TIES
Roll your untied ties rather than hang them. It allows the running stitch that constitutes the spine of the tie to relax. **ADD 5 YEARS.**

4. SHIRTS
Never dry-clean. Have them laundered and hand-ironed if possible. Less pressing means less wear and tear. **ADD 2 YEARS.**

5. SHOES
Own at least three good pairs for work. Never wear a pair more than twice a week. Use shoe trees. **ADD 20 YEARS.**

6. SUITS
Store your out-of-season suits in airtight bags. **ADD 5 YEARS.**

7. SUITS
Brush them regularly to remove lint in hidden areas, like armpits, that can attract moths. **ADD ANOTHER 2 YEARS.**

8. SUITS
Steam regularly to remove creases between annual dry cleaning. **ADD 10 YEARS.**

The Definitive Key to
CARE LABELS

What it means: Hand-wash. **What it really means:** Wash in warm water (between 90 and 105 degrees) mixed with detergent. Don't scrub too hard.

What it means: Do not iron. **What it really means:** Use a steamer to work out the wrinkles, or take it to a dry cleaner.

What it means: Do not tumble dry. **What it really means:** Drape the washed garment over a clothesline or a dry, clean surface that won't warp the garment's shape. Let dry.

What it means: Do not bleach. **What it really means:** Check your laundry detergent's ingredients for bleach's chemical name, sodium hypochlorite.

What it means: Dry-clean. **What it really means:** Always take delicate fabrics like silk to a dry cleaner. You can hand-wash some stuff yourself, but it's risky.

What it means: Machine-wash. **What it really means:** Number of dots indicates temperature. One is cold.

....

The *SARTORIAL CANON*

⧉ • ⧉

Your Wardrobe

....

BEXLEY ➧ This shoe manufacturer and retailer, founded in Lyon in 1985, has a rock-solid reputation in France for producing high-quality leather shoes at reasonable prices. But it's their red cedar shoe trees and hangers that have been lauded on blogs and Web sites stateside. www.bexley.com

THE INTERNATIONAL GUILD OF PROFESSIONAL BUTLERS ➧ What's the next step after securing the perfect wardrobe? Hiring a personal staff. The Guild's services include the recruitment and training worldwide of butlers, household managers, personal assistants, and others qualified to assist you with the chaos of your closet and schedule. If you haven't quite arrived, succumb to aspiration and peruse their Web site to learn about the "finer points of luxury and style," from napkin-folding to sherry sipping. www.butlersguild.com

SPACE BAG ➧ Sometimes, new technology trumps centuries-old tradition. When it comes to storing and protecting the suits in your closet, the watertight, nylon-and-polyethylene bags made by Space Bag will keep moths, dust, and humidity out better than canvas or plastic bags. They also compress, via a vacuum-seal, to save valuable space. www.spacebag.com

TUMI ➧ In the thirty years since Tumi's founding in 1975, the company's black ballistic nylon luggage has ferried countless businessmen's gear safely and stylishly around the globe. Tumi holds more than twenty-five patents for innovative design and engineering; in addition to its signature black travel bags, the company offers a wide variety of business accessories and luxury products. www.tumi.com